Heaven Knows!

Letters from Heaven and Hell to Ireland

BLACKWATER PRESS

ISBN 1 84131 490 0

Produced in Ireland by
Blackwater Press
c/o Folens Publishers
Hibernian Industrial Estate
Greenhills Road
Tallaght
Dublin 24

CONTENTS

FOREWORD

Which House drinks more, the Dáil or the Seanad? Which politician does not wear a wig? Which politician would like to wear a wig? What have Mary O'Rourke and Mother Teresa in common? What is the real story behind Charlie's Charvet shirts? What does Dev think of his granddaughter? Will David Norris become the next president of Ireland? Does Charlie McCreevy really have two or three sets of books? Is there life after Gay Byrne? Is BIFFO really a BIFFO? Keane – John B., Terry and Roy – together at last.

Only divine intervention could truly provide an answer to such searching Irish questions. Heaven Knows! provides not only the answers to these questions but raises many others that you were too nervous to ask. The power of prayer, positive thinking, Swiftian savagery and not a little wit combine in this book to prove that Dan Quayle was right when he said 'people that are really very weird can get into sensitive positions and have a tremendous impact on history'. In these pages you will meet many of these Irish 'characters'. Heaven knows we deserve them. But if they didn't exist would we really want to invent them? God bless and God save Ireland, because, if he doesn't, who will?

Letter from **Des Traynor**, accountant and Tribunal scapegoat, to
Ben Dunne, shopkeeper and financier to the Great and the Mighty:

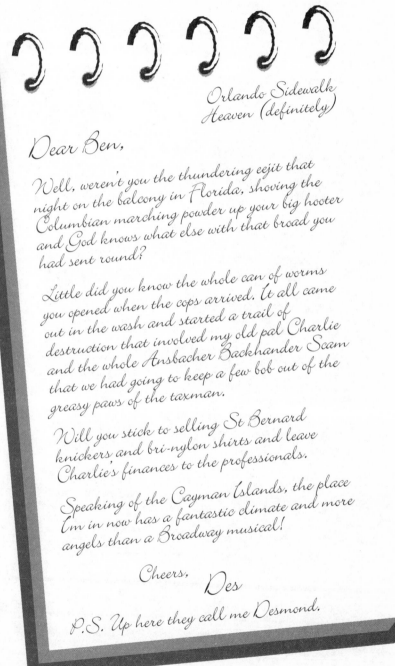

Orlando Sidewalk
Heaven (definitely)

Dear Ben,

Well, weren't you the thundering eejit that night on the balcony in Florida, shoving the Columbian marching powder up your big hooter and God knows what else with that broad you had sent round?

Little did you know the whole can of worms you opened when the cops arrived. It all came out in the wash and started a trail of destruction that involved my old pal Charlie and the whole Ansbacher Backhander Scam that we had going to keep a few bob out of the greasy paws of the taxman.

Will you stick to selling St Bernard knickers and bri-nylon shirts and leave Charlie's finances to the professionals.

Speaking of the Cayman Islands, the place I'm in now has a fantastic climate and more angels than a Broadway musical!

Cheers,
Des

P.S. Up here they call me Desmond.

1

From **John Millington Synge**, playwright and author of *The Playboy of the Western World*, to **Martin McDonagh**, playwright and author of *The Beauty Queen of Leenane*:

The Well of the Saints
Heaven

Dear Martin,

I'm destroyed with the hearing, since Tuesday was a week, of the fine plays you're after writing and how you have every female woman from Maam Cross to Scattery Island driven wild with the sultry looks and the millions you're after making at the playwrighting and you hardly out of the cradle.

One recent arrival here told me how he saw your play The Crippled Beauty Queen of Leenane in the Lonesome West and that, fair play to you, you pulled out every stop and sent the Dublin middle-class audience reeling into the night after two and a half hours of murder and mayhem and crusty bachelors and frustrated spinsters, and that you had set Anna Manahan up for life playing the best sitting-down role she ever had and she to be a star from Bohola to Broadway.

Don't mind the begrudgers who ask what you know about Ireland, anyway, you to be born and reared in Kilburn High Street and you set to writing your plays only after hearing your cousins talking like that and, drinking and fighting and killing one another on your summer holidays in Leenane. Didn't I write the best plays with my ear to a chink in the floor, listening to the servant girls in the house where I was lodging in the Aran Islands?

My life on you boy, and you'll discover, too, that there's a grave difference between a gallous story and seeing your name in lights. Like Christy Mahon, aren't you the buckleppin', swaggerin' and very newest Playboy of the Western World?

John Millington Synge

Micheál Mac Liammóir – actor, artist and founder of The Gate Theatre – writes to **Michael Colgan**, artistic director of The Gate Theatre:

Pearly Gate
Heaven

My dear Michael,

For years I did a one-man show all over the world called The Importance of Being Earnest. Now I see you are doing your own one-man show all over the world called The Earnestness of Being Important!

I must confess, I find all this wallowing in Beckett and Pinter quite unhealthy, however fashionable it may be. Oh, for an evening of frocks and fobs at The Gate, with young men you know who can sport a smoking jacket and young gels who can wear pearls and hold a cigarette holder at the right angle.

All this squabbling about money with The Arts Council I find quite unhealthy. Dear Hilton and I never had that problem: we simply never had it to squabble about! We put on the plays, the audiences came and the politics we left to Leinster House.

We'll see you at the Pearly Gate, dear boy, where there's a cast of thousands and a divine show that will run for eternity – if you get past the box office!

Micheál

From **Oliver St John Gogarty** – senator, poet, wit – to
Ulick O'Connor, poet, playwright, pugilist:

Wit's End
Heaven

Dear Ulick,

Some are born great, some have
greatness thrust upon them and then
there's yourself, dear boy! What are we
going to do with you at all? Someone
brought up a copy of your published
diaries, and I haven't seen so many
dropped names since Maud Gonne
was a girl! Imagine all those famous
people were bit players in your hectic
life! Hilton and Michael and Marianne
and Mariga and Desmond and
Brendan and Myles – all touched by
your wit and charm and genius!
Fair play to you, the version of my
own hectic life and times you wrote
was good, but did you have to try to
re-live it yourself in a minor key? You
dabbled and dribbled and did the
longest one-man show in Irish history:
The Importance of Being Me!
Indeed, Ulick, it's true what they say:
you never had an unspoken or
unpublished thought!

Yours, agog with apathy, awaiting
your arrival,

Oliver St John Gogarty

Kitty O'Shea, controversial mistress and later wife of Charles Stewart Parnell, writes to Taoiseach Bertie Ahern's partner, **Celia Larkin**:

Cypress Grove
Heaven

Dear Celia,

For the love and honour of God and the sake of the Party of Truth and Justice, which are going to be in power for the rest of yours and Bertie's lives, will you grab that man by the mane and tell him to piss or get off the pot. If he doesn't make an honest woman of you, threaten to turn that Farmleigh pile into a Makeover and Colour Me Beautiful Daycare Centre for Ex-nuns.

I never took any claptrap from my man, Parnell, and as my old drinking pal, John Wayne, said to me over a few Jack Daniels in the Celestial Karaoke Bar, 'If you've got them by the balls, their minds and hearts will follow'.

Yours in anticipation (but not buying the hat yet!),

Kitty

Seán McEntee, former Finance Minister, considers the position of the Finance Minister, **Charlie McCreevy:**

High Finance Corner
Heaven

Dear Mr McCreevy,

Let me be brief, for I fear to be anything else might jeopardise my hold on your concentration. I am in awe of your style. You keep three sets of figures: one to confuse the public, another to confuse the Cabinet and a yet another to confuse yourself.

Most impressive.

Yours very sincerely,

Seán McEntee

P.S. What do you favour for Cheltenham next year? Ten bob on Charlie's Angel, or a euro on Celia's Wedding?

P.P.S. Who was the last Minister for Finance to become Taoiseach? Was it Ruairí Quinn? (Where is he now? Out shooting Rabbittes, I suppose.) No, it was Bertie, of course; he did it his way. Be humble and learn from your Boss or else you will be the next (last?) Minister for Defence (Minister for War).

Letter from Count **John McCormack**, Irish tenor,
to **The Celtic Tenors**:

Chorus Angelorum
Heaven

My hearty boyos!

I'm taking a break from delighting God with
'Panis Angelicus' to say a few things to
you young bucks. I have heard it rumoured
that you are carrying on that glorious
tradition of the Irish Tenor – which single-
handedly I invented and promoted –
wherever Irish doleful dirges are known and
mangled the world over.

Of course, in the days before satellite
television and this place called The Point, I
sang before a million adoring fans at The
Eucharistic Congress in The Phoenix Park
in 1932. In Carnegie Hall in New York,
there wasn't a dry seat in the house when I
sang 'I Hear You Calling Me'. Indeed the
Music Critic of the New York Times in his
review said: 'When John Mc Cormack hit

high C in Carnegie Hall last night, you couldn't get a tram ticket between the cheeks of his royal Irish arse!'

Look at you! It takes three of you poncing around amid a ton of amplifiers and speakers as you mangle 'Danny Boy' yet again. It used to be known as The Art of Bel Canto but you have invented The Age of Can Belto.

Boys, will you give up your caterwauling and crawthumping! Give back the flashy tuxedos and shiny shoes. On second thoughts, hold onto them because there is a new bar in Manhattan called The Lost Chord.

Yours, in staves and crotchets,

Count John McCormack,
Papal Knight,
God's Own Gloria in Excelsis

Samuel Beckett, morose Irish playwright and novelist, writes to **Edna O'Brien**, novelist and Irishwoman:

Lower Depths
Elysium

My Dear Edna,

I have been waiting here with Godot a long time, but all we get is long silence at the end of a long day, past all caring. Time she stopped. I can't go on! I must go on! Edna, how you do go on!

You looked lovely as ever on *The Late Late Show* with Pat Kenny, slavering at the mouth and trying to peep down your cleavage. You were indeed the personification of Mother Ireland as you sighed long and hard, tossed your burnished auburn hair and looked longingly into the television camera lens. Not only Mother Ireland but Deirdre of the Sorrows, Queen Maeve, Granuaile, Cathleen Ní Houlihan and the Sean Bhean Bhocht.

Like Maud Gonne you brought comfort to the brave republican prisoners in jails North and South. You have dined for Ireland in cold marquees on the White House Lawn on St Patrick's Day. You have gone deep into The Dark Woods where terrible secrets lurk and brought them screaming out into the glare of arc lights and international network television.

Remember and celebrate all the dead voices. About the God you railed and ranted against in Catholic Ireland, He does not exist! When you eventually deign to grace Heaven, assumed body and soul from the Burren into a clear azure sky, you will join the waiting Godot and myself to live out our happy days.

Time I stopped. I switch off. Make sense who may.

Yours, Sam

To **Maeve Binchy**, Irish author extraordinaire, from **Dale Carnegie**, author of *How to Win Friends and Influence People*:

Carnegie Hall
Heaven

Dear Maeve,

A good friend of yours who has come on up here ahead of you asked me to drop you a line to suggest a few ways in which you might begin to overcome your crippling shyness and debilitating inferiority complex.

Now, Maeve, as a writer you know you will have to go on radio and television and be interviewed in public. When you write in your isolated garret you are fine, but when you go out in public, as you must, you will have to make conversation and try to work up some little anecdotes and stories to amuse and entertain people. You can't stand there like a duck in thunder! You must try to get out more, however it goes against the grain of your hermit's nature. Travel more, learn to lip read, mix more.

Set yourself goals, Maeve. Take a trip down the country on the Lilac Bus. Cultivate a Circle of Friends. Get your lovely husband Gordon to take you out for a meal at Quentin's trendy restaurant, where you can promptly ignore him and eavesdrop to your heart's content on the couple at the next table who are having a storming row.

Enrol in a night class or join a prayer group and Light A Penny Candle. Watch Oprah Winfrey on television and see how that nice woman manages always to find something positive to say about everyone. To help you with your crippling shyness, learn the trick of talking on the in breath as well as the out.

Develop a firm handshake, look people straight in the eye, walk tall. Stop saying 'I don't know what to say about that. Ask Gordon'. Look at Joe Duffy and Maureen Gaffney on radio and television. (On second thoughts, better not!)

Remember, the longest journey starts with one step. You can collect these and other priceless fridge-magnet gems when you enrol in The Dale Carnegie Institute for the Boring and the Bewildered.

Have a nice life!

Dale Carnegie

To President **Mary McAleese** from **Eamon de Valera**, former Taoiseach and President:

A Mháire, a chroí,

I have been following with great interest your meteoric rise to sainthood and expect that any day now you will be joining myself and Sinéad in celestial surroundings, having been assumed body and soul from the site of the Papal Cross in the Phoenix Park on a fine Sunday in May. As you are swept upwards you will look down on your beloved Four Green Fields and consider how you have presided for seven years over the glorious triumph of what started out as the Celtic Tiger and has now, alas, become Bertie's Badger.

Maybe one day again we will hear the innocent laughter of comely maidens dancing at the crossroads, replacing the projectile puking of stag parties defiling the night in Temple Bar. Soon, with the help of God and Our Lady of Knock, we will see the blue-and-white-veiled Legion of Mary winding its way past the vile dens of whorehouses and lap-dancing clubs.

No more will the sex-crazed youth of Ireland go backpacking to the vice dens of Bangkok or Sydney, where they sell their souls for a line of coke and a mobile phone. Let them repair to the Gaeltacht, where they will dance The Siege of Ennis and aspire to open guest-houses called Dun na Rí. Our four green fields will once more resound to the wholesome laughter, lively lilting and sean nós singing of our people, instead of the effeminate poncing of the latest Louis Walsh Boyband.

Mise, i ndochas agus grá,

Eamon de Valera

14

From **W. B. Yeats**, Nobel Poet Laureate, to **Seamus Heaney**, Nobel Poet Laureate:

Poet's Corner
Heaven

You should arise and go now
and go to Tennessee
And a large fortune make there
at the University.
Nine doctorates will you have
there and a series on TV
And you'll live and grow grey
there until 2023.

And you shall be revered there,
for always night and day,
For poetry and punditry Famous
Seamus is au fait.
There midnight's all a-glimmer
with champagne and repartee
With the Kennedys, McCourts,
Clintons and Tom Fee.

You should arise and go now and
go to Tennessee
For Ireland is alright for bogs and
churning sea,
But a Nobel call is beckoning to
bestride a bigger stage
Where Famous Seamus digs for gold
with every poem on page.

Her Late Majesty, **Elizabeth the Queen Mother**, writes to His Royal Highness **Charles, Prince of Wales**:

Royal Box

My dear Charles,

I do so apologise for not having written sooner, but it would appear that things are ordered here rather differently than one was lead to believe by dear Nanny and, indeed, successive Archbishops of Canterbury. For one thing, servants are quite unknown here and, as a consequence, one must attend to every little thing (such as day-to-day correspondence) oneself! Thank goodness it is quite unseasonably warm at present, or one would be obliged to light one's own fire. It seems that your dear mother's writ as head of the Anglican Church on Earth does not quite extend to the hereafter.

Another most trying consequence is that it is quite impossible to get a gin and Cinzano at all before 3 pm (let alone a decent cocktail - a fact, as I am sure you will appreciate, that has quite discommoded your dear Aunt Margaret!). As for any decent horse-racing: well, suffice it to say there is no shortage of book-makers but not a single race run since one arrived here. Quite intolerable, really.

Your Aunt Margaret has fallen in with what one can only describe as quite a fast set - quelle surprise, as those appalling Frenchmen are wont to say. One has seen very

16

little of your late (and ex) wife, Diana. Rumour has it that she is leading a campaign to abolish 'Fire and Brimstone', whatever they may be. Quite unsuitable behaviour for a Royal (or even an ex-Royal), don't you agree? Such a pity that you have even less influence over the gel now than ever you did before she was gathered unto 'God (who calls himself 'Nick', apparently).

Speaking of matters connubial, one is led to believe that you are still planning to marry that Parker-Bowles woman. My dear Charles, I quite forbid it! One's sources indicate that the creature is practically a Catholic and there are quite enough of them here to put one off them for life (or eternity). The only good thing about them is that they are even more miserable here than oneself.

Well, one really must go in search of a little snifter before one expires from thirst (if such a thing is possible). Still, it's being so cheerful as keeps one going!

Your ever-loving,

Granny

P.S. Do tell your poor mother that she behaved very badly over Diana's butler. I mean to say, dear boy, she wouldn't forget the dog's dinner now, would she?

Letter from **Eamon de Valera** to an Taoiseach, **Bertie Ahern**, TD:

High Moral Ground
Heaven

Taoiseach,

I suppose I should be grateful that, at last, you have taken your lead from myself and come to the realisation that further sacrifice of money would now be in vain. Political victory must be allowed to rest for the moment with those who have destroyed the Bertie Bowl. However, it gives me no satisfaction to know that it has taken you, my successor, so long to acknowledge when you have been beaten.

If I made one mistake in life, it was to utter the words: 'Whenever I wanted to know what the Irish people wanted, I had only to examine my own heart and it told me straight away.' Not that it wasn't true in my case, but everyone who has followed me as leader of the Irish nation seems to believe that merely sitting in my seat gives him the same insight. Taoiseach, if you learn one lesson from this farce, let it be that you are NOT I and, as a consequence, if you should need to know what the Irish people want, you should ASK them what they want.

Of course, if you do not get the right answer from them the first time, you can always ask them again. And again, if necessary.

But I see you have already followed that last advice. Maith an buachaill!

Le meas,
Eamon de Valera

An **unknown poet muses** in Heaven on the **Charles Haughey** Charvet shirt controversy. The poem is read in a Dublin accent just like that of Mr Brennan the bread man:

Shirty Corner
Heaven

The Tale of a Charvet Shirt

Let me tell you a little story
About the Charvet shirt
The idea came from Terry
But Charlie took the hurt.

After champagne at the Ritz
Terry was feeling angry
So she says to C J H,
'Your shirts don't make me randy.

'I know a famous shirt shop
Just down the very next Rue
The shirts are trez expensive
They're much more me than you'.

So off they went to Charvet
Where Charlie spent a pack
On shirts and ties and underwear
To get Terry on her back.

The rest is now just history
McCracken, Flood and all
The lawyers are wearing Charvet
And Charlie awaits the call.

Terry's packed her bags
For the South of France
Full of shirts and ties and underwear
And not a bloody word of thanks!

Letter from **Eamon Andrews**, father of Irish broadcasting, to **Gay Byrne,** superstar and agony aunt to the Irish nation:

Television Club
Heaven

My dear Gay,

I bet you never expected to hear from me again! I hope the shock doesn't send you into a sad decline! Gay, old friend, what the hell is going on in RTÉ? We don't often get to listen to the wireless or watch the TV up here but, when we do, frankly I'm embarrassed for Ireland. The radio is bad enough with David Hanly growling the nation to wakefulness of a morning and Val Joyce sending them into a coma in the evening (not to mention Joe Duffy out-Mollying Molly Malone and John Creedon attempting to be the nicest person on the planet five bloody days a week). But Jaysus, Gay, the telly! What happened to it?

You and I were there at the beginning. It wasn't easy getting it started, as I'm sure you remember. I'm pretty certain that trying to get the Department of Finance to cough up the money for the studio, four lights, a camera and an operator contributed to my early demise. But, by God, when we had it done, it was worth watching. When Charles Mitchell read the news, everyone knew it was serious news. Anne Doyle is easy on the eye but she's too damn cheerful. Pat Kenny sounds alright on the radio but sure he's miles better than Gerry Kelly on the box (admit it Gay).

Gay, there's only one man (alive) that can save the day! Put down that golf club, get offa that Harley Davidson and get yourself back to Montrose. Your station and your nation (and my blushes) need you!

Love to Kay and the kids!

Eamon

P.S. Russell Murphy sends his regards. He said he was glad he left Ireland before the CAB was established. Do you think he really spent (invested) all your money?

From footballing superhero **Roy of the Rovers** to footballing prima donna **Roy Keane**:

Dear Roy,

I, too, was once the stuff of schoolboy dreams: the Striker who never let the team or the fans down, the cool, clean hero who showed his skill and mastery, on and off the pitch. Melchester Rovers Ruled OK; men were gods and the fans adored us. With my beloved wife, Penny Laine, I ruled the roost long before Posh and Becks flaunted themselves in Hello magazine. We were King and Queen and we reigned with pride.

Now, Roy, you once inhabited the high moral ground and gave boys and girls, grown men and women and toothless wonders a reason to get out of bed on a Saturday morning – or to travel to the Land of the Rising Sun to exult in the fighting spirit of the Boys in Green.

But, oh how the mighty are fallen. You skulked in your tent like an Irish Achilles, all wounded pride and attitude. Sure, there were things to put right, reasons to complain. But you must realise that football is a team game and that you are only one of a body of men. As the wise poet John Donne said long ago, 'No man is an island'. We are all part of the mainland. No one man can call the tune or set the agenda.

Roy, it is never too late to come to your senses, to climb back up on your rightful pedestal with pride and dignity. We all want you back there. Let our children and grandchildren remember you as a flawed hero with feet of gold – feet that once briefly turned to clay but returned to their rightful gold.

Put your best foot forward, man, walk out on the pitch of life, with your head held high. Be proud you were proved right, magnanimous in victory and a giant among pygmies.

Roy of the Rovers

P.S. Genesis – The Book of Revelations – confirmed that what you said to Tommy Gorman was correct. Now do the honourable thing and captain the Irish team in a testimonial match for Mick McCarthy and Brendan Menton.

John Healy, former *Irish Times* correspondent, Eurocrat and defender of the West of Ireland against Dublin suburban imperialism, writes to **John Waters**, *Irish Times* columnist and defender of the West of Ireland against Dublin suburban imperialism:

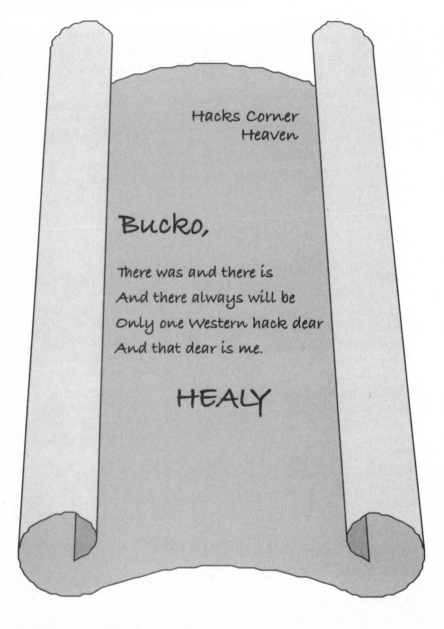

Hacks Corner
Heaven

Bucko,

There was and there is
And there always will be
Only one Western hack dear
And that dear is me.

HEALY

Al Capone, who never needed any introduction, writes to **Ray Burke**, who may well be in need of introductions:

Gangsters Corner
Hell

Dear Rambo, my friend,

There's always room at the top, baby – after the investigation's over. Can't recall who said that, but in my experience it's good advice.

I know a thing or two about corruption, which is why I've been sweatin' trying to read the No.1 best-seller, the Floodgate findings. All on your behalf, of course. Men of our stature are always victims in a society which lacks imagination, Ray baby. You were done for stuffed envelopes; I was done for stuffing my enemies. I tell ya, Ray, there's a lot to be said for the quick-fix solution. Who's this P.J. Mara guy? I like the sound of him. Put a violin case in that guy's hands and send him off on a mission, that's what old Al advises.

I don't want you rottin' away in the Joy (like Liam Lawlor), so I think you should take the old slow boat to Spain with your loot and sit it out until the heat is off. Maybe that nice builder who looked after you could build you a hacienda, where you can collect your well-earned pension and wait until the call comes from the backbenchers for you to oust Bertie and lead your party to overall victory. You can then dissolve the Tribunals and get back to business.

Yours in all sincerity,

And in haste,

Al Capone

P.S. Have you any idea why the CAB are looking for me?
P.P.S. Is there any difference between Hell and the Tribunals? In Hell things are hot all the time; in the Tribunals things are only getting hot.

From the black and white minstrels to **Enda Kenny**, leader of the Fine Gael Party:

Uncle Tom's Cabin
Heaven

(To be sung by Jim Mitchell
to banjo accompaniment)

Eenie Meenie Minie Moe
Catch a leader by the toe
If he squeals let him go
Eenie Meenie Minie Moe.

Eenie Meenie Minie Moe
Catch a hack by the toe
If he leaks let him go
Eenie Meenie Minie Moe.

Eenie Meenie Minie Moe
Catch a doctor by the toe
If he spins let him go
Eenie Meenie Minie Moe

Eenie Meenie Minie Moe
Catch the voters by the toe
If they defect let them go
Eenie Meenie Minie Moe.

Judy Garland, singer and actress, to **Mary Coughlan**, singer and blues expert:

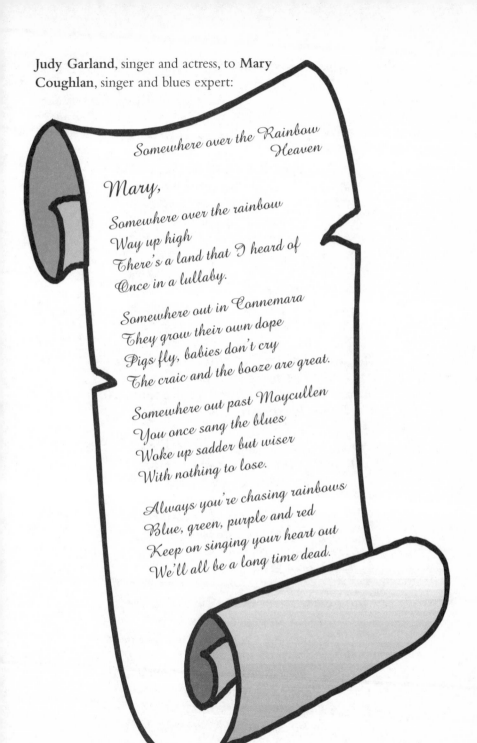

Somewhere over the Rainbow
Heaven

Mary,

Somewhere over the rainbow
Way up high
There's a land that I heard of
Once in a lullaby.

Somewhere out in Connemara
They grow their own dope
Pigs fly, babies don't cry
The craic and the booze are great.

Somewhere out past Moycullen
You once sang the blues
Woke up sadder but wiser
With nothing to lose.

Always you're chasing rainbows
Blue, green, purple and red
Keep on singing your heart out
We'll all be a long time dead.

Patrick Kavanagh, poet, addresses the Standing Army of Irish Poets 2002:

*A Canal Bank Seat
Heaven*

*On Raglan Road on an autumn day
I sought a grant and Aosdána too
A bursary, a flight for free
A wealthy widow to serve me tea.
I saw the dangers yet I walked
In poverty and penury
And I said let grief be a fallen leaf
And a weekly spot on TV3.*

*On Grafton Street in November
Past McDonald's, Marks and Sparks
The buskers play, the crowds all pay
The Celtic Tiger purrs – what larks!
The Tart with the Cart still plies her wares
But I'm dying for a cup of tay
I'm a long way now from the harrow and plough
Tarry Flynn, Green Fool and me.*

*From Iniskeen I came up with a dream
To tell it straight from my own heart
But poverty and misery
Were bedfellows from the start.
I saw the danger yet I walked
With Behan, Clarke and Kiely.
Had I known then what I know now
I'd have lived the life of Reilly.*

*On a quiet street where old ghosts meet
I'm a stranger in this city
With lap-dancing clubs and all-night pubs
Where the poor and sad get no pity.
But I have woo'd not as I should
Never got a penny's pay
But as a man grows old his poems grow gold
At the dawning of the day.*

From **James Joyce**, author, to **Dublin City Council**:

Lofty Heights
Seventh Heaven

Gentlemen,

It has been said that if Dublin city were to be razed to the ground it could all be rebuilt in exact detail by studying the pages of my novel Ulysses. You, gentlemen, bring that destruction one step nearer every day by your actions – or indeed lack of action. From swerve of shore to bend of bay you seem determined to allow pollution, congestion, demolition and devastation to rule and you seem destined to preside over the annihilation of this once-proud city.

Virgil once wrote, 'If you seek a monument, look around you'. It is fitting that the Spike in O'Connell Street stands like a piercing dagger through the heart of Anna Livia.

Yours in disgust,

James Joyce

Oscar Wilde, dramatist and wit, writes to Graham Norton, TV chat show host:

Pink Power Corner
Heaven

My Dear Boy,

I once said, to great acclaim, that to love oneself was the beginning of a lifelong romance. In your case, young man, you have also proved another dictum of mine, namely, that being natural is such a difficult pose to keep up. How I wish I had lived long enough to appear on this new-fangled television, although in your case five nights a week seems, as Lady Bracknell might say, somewhat excessive.

It seems a great shame, dear boy, that you have not used this magic invention of television to re-invent the salon. You could have turned your hour of vulgarity and banality into a bastion of sparkling wit, good conversation and made it the talk of the town and the delight of nations.

Instead of carefully honed epigrams, shimmering paradoxes dripping from the lips of Dorian Grays, what do you give us five nights a week? We have to endure a clapped-out Joan Collins or some starlet from Eastenders and I'm A Celebrity – Get Me Out Of Here!

Some of your guests resemble the unspeakable in full pursuit of the unutterable. No wonder the entire population of your native Bandon squirms in unison every time you burst upon their screens. The poor things are forced to ring Joe Duffy as a helpline. You have proved, beyond all reasonable doubt, that in the question of taste nothing succeeds like excess.

Your, in mortification,

Oscar Wilde

From **Fred Astaire**, dancer, to **Michael Flatley**, dancer:

The Ballroom of Romance
Stairway to Heaven

Dear Michael,

You know what? Here amid the heavenly chorus line they say that you always wanted to hoof it in a big Broadway show but that you were hampered by one big drawback – when you went on stage you were always afraid of stairs. (Fred Astaire's – G'ddit? Oh, forget it!)

My source here tells me that you are hanging up your steel toecaps, tight leather jeans and glistening body lotion. What a pity! There was a time when you could burn up the stage, when you liberated Irish dance from the stale and staid 'Back Like a Wooden Board/Ankles Like Wet Lettuce School' as you strode across the stage like a Colossus. Too many nights on the Casting Couch of Lillie's Bordello and Reynards have transformed you from International Lord of the Dance into a swaggering Lord of the Manor in Cork.

Step it out once more and show them you can still hoof it with the best. Broadway babes will love you and chorus lines adore you. Step it out there, Michael, and show them you're the only man who can fill my patent shoes!

Your in step, heel and toe,

Fred

P.S. Did you know that Mike Murphy won a world medal for lap...sorry, tap-dancing – do you know Mike?

Lady **Hazel Lavery**, wife of Sir John and former ornament of the pre-euro Irish currency, writes to **Sinéad O'Connor** of her ideal Irishman:

Mistresses Corner,
Heaven

Dear Sinéad,

Some clever person once said: 'If the authorities warn you of the dangers of sex, there is one important lesson to be learned. Do not have sex with the authorities.'

In my day, there was the dashing Michael Collins. Now he was forever dashing in and out of my bed at Cromwell Road. I don't know how we ever got the Treaty signed what with all the dashing. Then there was the sensitive, Kevin O'Higgins, what a darling boy. I like my men to be like a paper handkerchief - strong, soft and disposable. God knows I disposed of a few in my time. But then you have disposed of a few yourself.

Were you delighted that John Waters was not made editor of The Irish Times. But then again, maybe the children's allowance might have been increased. Not that you need the money, Sinéad. You are a sensible girl with your own income and a will of iron. Did you ever get an allowance from the Catholic Church when you became a bishop? I imagine they took fearful exception to you tearing up the picture of the Pope on television. I though it was great gas altogether. Now what was it Dr Paisley called the Pope? 'That slanderous celibate who lives on the banks of the Tiber.' There was nothing celibate about me, Sinéad, except perhaps to sell a bit here and sell a bit there! Well, darling, keep up the good work, and never mind the begrudgers.

Much love,
Yours ever,
Hazel

Letter from **St Joseph**, carpenter and foster parent, to **John Waters**, journalist and single parent:

The Stables
Heaven

Dear John,

It may come as some surprise to you to learn that, here in Paradise, we are avid readers of your columns in The Irish Times. Naturally, given my role as foster father to Our Saviour and Lord, I have paid particular attention to your writings on the subject of the rights of single fathers everywhere.

During my time in the Vale of Tears, I thought the dual roles imposed on me of protector of the honour of Mary and foster father to her Child were more than any man should have to bear. Indeed, the trials and tribulations of having an Archangel as a father-in-law (so to speak) and a saintly virgin as a betrothed seemed, at the time, unreasonable to say the least.

However, a brief perusal of your articles in The Irish Times (which I read on the Internet every day) over what seems to be aeons has led me to the belief that yours is the heavier cross to bear. I mean, Sinéad O'Connor?? I thought I was hard done by to have the Virgin Immaculate as a life partner, but you, poor thing, had to put up with a bishop, a lesbian and a pop-singer. And she having torn up a poster of his Holiness the Pope! Did she ever tear up a photograph of you?

Rest assured that you are in my thoughts!

Best regards,

St Joseph

31

Text message from **Christy Ring**, hurler,
to **Pelé**, footballer and Viagra spokesman:

Text message from **Sir Thomas Beecham**, conductor,
to **Jean Butler**, Irish dancer:

Letter from **Job**, prophet, to **Mick McCarthy**, football manager:

Dear Mick,

You said you resigned as international manager for the good of the team. Fair play, you put the team first. Did you put the team first when you sent Ireland's best player home from the World Cup? OK, so he said awful things about you — he even called you a muppet. Did he burn your sheep, did he kill your fine sons, did he scarify you with visions? No, he just called you names. Names, schnames. What names were you called from the terraces in Millwall?

Mick, now that it is all over, it's time to move on. Life is strange and what goes around comes around. Remember Job had patience (something the Irish ain't noted for): you must also be patient and wait — you will have the last laugh.

What will be the public reaction when Keane returns to the international team and they lose every match? There will be a chorus of BBM (Bring Back Mick). Since Eamon Dunphy once played for Milwall, this qualifies him to be the new Irish manager but would he do any better (OK, he is a good author and pundit, but he was never much of a player).

Mick, when you become manager of Manchester United you can insist on Roy calling you Mr McCarthy — 'ouch'.

Your patient friend,

Job

Frank Sinatra, American singer, to **Charles J. Haughey**, former Taoiseach:

Charlie,

And now the end is near
And you must face the final curtain,
You'll state your case of which you're certain.
You've lived a live that's full,
You've travelled each and every highway,
And more, much more than that,
You did it your way.

Regrets, you've had a few
But far too few to get upset with.
You've had trials and tribunals
Not enough rain to get wet with.
You've done the state some service
Or shall we say you've done the state!
But more, much more than that
You did it your way.

Now you look out across Kinsealy
With hooded eyes a little bleary.
The world was once your oyster
When you hung round with crooks and shysters.
The shirts, champagne and Terry
Seem like a dream that's gone unfairly
But more, much more than this
You did it your way.

P.S. You should record this song on my new
label Tribunal Records. You do the singing; get
Mara to play the fiddle and drums. It'll be No.1
both on Earth and in Heaven.
P.P.S. Good news – you are never going to die,
so organsie another comeback.

Andy Warhol, American artist and film maker, to the inhabitants of the Big Brother house, boy bands, celebrity chat show hosts, all wannabes, starlets, nymphettes, supermodels and Louis Walsh:

STUDIO 54
HELL

HI ALL,

ONCE UPON A TIME IN THE U S OF A, I SAID: 'IN THE FUTURE EVERYBODY WILL BE FAMOUS FOR FIFTEEN MINUTES.' LITTLE DID I KNOW HOW PROPHETIC THAT REMARK MIGHT BE! I HAD MY OWN FIFTEEN MINUTES IN THE SUN AND MADE MY MARK, EVEN IF I WAS FAMOUS ONLY FOR BEING FAMOUS! NOW IT SEEMS THAT ANYBODY WHO HAS BEEN PHOTOGRAPHED MORE THAN THREE TIMES IS A CELEBRITY. NEW YORK, LONDON, PARIS, EVEN CORK, GALWAY AND DUBLIN, ARE FULL OF PEOPLE ALL TRYING FRANTICALLY TO BE FAMOUS — ALL LIVING LIVES OF VERY LOUD DESPERATION!

HERE IN HELL, IT'S FULL OF PEOPLE WHO USED TO BE SOMEBODY. HERE THE NEXT BEST THING IS YESTERDAY'S MAN. FAME IS BOTH THE SPUR AND THE NOOSE. HERE THEY HAVE LEARNED TOO LATE THAT LIFE IS NOT A REHEARSAL BUT THE REAL THING. ON THE STAGE OF LIFE, YOU'RE ON AND, BABY, YOU'RE ON YOUR OWN!

YOURS ANONYMOUSLY,

ANDY WARHOL

Sigmund Freud, psychiatrist, writes to **Dr Anthony Clare**, psychiatrist and television personality:

The Couch
Heaven

Dear Dr Clare,

I have been asked to write up some case notes on your behaviour of recent, which has been causing some concern to your colleagues and even some patients at St Patrick's Hospital.

From reports I hear that you have developed, in recent years, a peculiar and somewhat rare form of mania, entitled Recurrent Media Obsessive Behaviour. This manifests itself in an inability to restrain oneself from making statements or passing pronouncements on radio and television, in newspapers and magazines, learned journals or Ireland's Own and The Sacred Heart Messenger on such diverse topics as the male menopause, coping with fame, delusions of adequacy and Mad Cow Disease. So addicted are you to pronouncements before cameras that it is reported that every time you open the fridge door and the little light goes on, you do twenty minutes!

The only cure for this intolerable and very distressing condition — especially for your viewers — is that you are given your own series on television, where you can rest assured that nobody is watching you. Or if they are they have only tuned in to catch the babes who read the news and have no interest your witterings, with you banging on about life and death and the whole damn thing.

Yours, id, ego and summa laude,
                    Freud

From **Edith Piaf**, chanteuse and legend, to **Marianne Faithfull**, singer and legend:

Moulin Rouge
Heaven

Non, Rien de rien ...
Non, je ne regrette rien,
Ni le bien qu'on ma fait,
Ni le mal. Tout ca m'est bien egal!

No, no regrets
Let you have no regrets
You have lived life to the full
Full of faith to the last
To you the torch song has passed.

Among your souvenirs
Do not shed any tears
You've survived all the jeers
And a born again career.

No, no regrets
For the world won't forget.
Have a nice cup of tea
And a Mars bar at three
And you'll have no regrets.

No, no regrets
You've come round once again
Once you were a vamp
Now you're quite camp
And an icon in slane.

T. S. Eliot, poet, addresses **Paul Durcan**, poet:

Prufrock Pastures
Heaven

Let us go then you and I
When the evening is spread out against the sky
And the audience etherised and bored right rigid.
Over a simple and humble repast
Let us talk of Ireland past
When every second girl was christened Brigid.

In the room the women come and go
Wondering how long this poetry reading can possibly go on
And when the bar is closing and if there is any chance of a party in
Ringsend.

Now the barman's calling time
But you've just begun to rhyme
About the Kilfenora Teaboy and the Boyne.
Should you go out for a smoke
Or chance lighting up a toke
Or chance making love outside Áras an Uachtaráin in the dark?

And in the room the women come and go
Wondering what it would be like to bed a poet
And if you faked would he turn over and not know it?

He grows old, he grows old
He shouldn't wear so much gold
And that hair brushed forward is getting very thin.
He should wear white flannel trousers and walk on Ringsend beach
Where he'll hear the sirens singing each to each.

Now from the locked room the women cannot go
There's no escaping now this woeful woe
And tomorrow night he's on The Late Late Show!

38

Sir Noel Coward, playwright and genius, addresses **Mrs Shaw**, theatrical mother of Fiona Shaw, actress:

Don't put your daughter on the stage, Mrs Shaw,
Don't put your daughter on the stage;
She'll lose her Cork accent, and start sounding very posh,
She'll play bloody-minded Greeks and in Hollywood make dosh
But what if the Cork neighbours think it's tosh?
Don't put your daughter on the stage.

Don't put your daughter on the stage, Mrs Shaw,
Don't put your daughter on the stage.
Her Medea and Electra may elevate her career
But what if she comes home and swans about just
    like King Lear
Expiring on the heath and filling everyone with Fear?
Don't put your daughter on the stage.

Don't put your daughter on the stage, Mrs Shaw,
Don't put your daughter on the stage.
Driven by the fates to mutilate her father
Never to lead the boy-next-door in white up to the altar
Living with other luvvies with your photo in the Troc
Your Lady Macbeth in the nude
    giving everyone a shock!
Please, Mrs Shaw,
Don't let your daughter rove
Keep her in Cobh
Encourage her to fall in love
    But don't let your daughter on the stage!

39

From **Sir Winston Churchill**, statesman and historian, to **Tony Blair**, aspiring statesman and British prime minister:

Old Boy's Club
Heaven

Dear Blair,

In one of my finer speeches to the House of Commons, just after the war, in 1947, I said that the English never draw a line without blurring it. Now in these dark days, at a time when you should be acting like prime minister with nerves of steel and balls of iron, you are incapable of drawing a line without <u>Blairing</u> it. In global terms you have become a political whore on the international stage, prepared to go to war or bed with whatever madman can show you the biggest weapon.

You are, indeed, a modest little man with a lot to be modest about. There is nothing more pathetic than a sheep in sheep's clothing masquerading as a ram. Or, to alter the metaphor, a lapdog to President George's mongrel Rottweiler.

Never in the field of human conflict have so many owed so little to so few for their warmongering. So, if the dogs of war are let loose you must not complain that your American presidential ally is barking mad. All that is left to you in your tainted and discredited role as the Lapdog Prime Minister is to fight them with the sound-bite, to blind them with the photo-call, to blast them with megaphone diplomacy and to scatter the ashes of your once promising career to the four winds.

Churchill

From **Attila the Hun,** the former scourge of Europe, to **Saddam Hussein,** the tyrant of the Middle East:

You make me feel so young;
I'm just Attila the Hun.
You have them on the run,
Laughing in the sun!

You look out from a gun,
Mass destruction every one.
You're a disaster, not much fun
And Bush and Blair won't turn.

You make me look okay,
Bin Laden kneels to pray,
Islam will have its sway
The dawning of a new day.

So sing along with Saddam's song,
The sheikh who can do no wrong.
We're marching to an oil drum gong,
A beat that goes on and on.

William Blake, poet, writes to Tiger Woods, golfer:

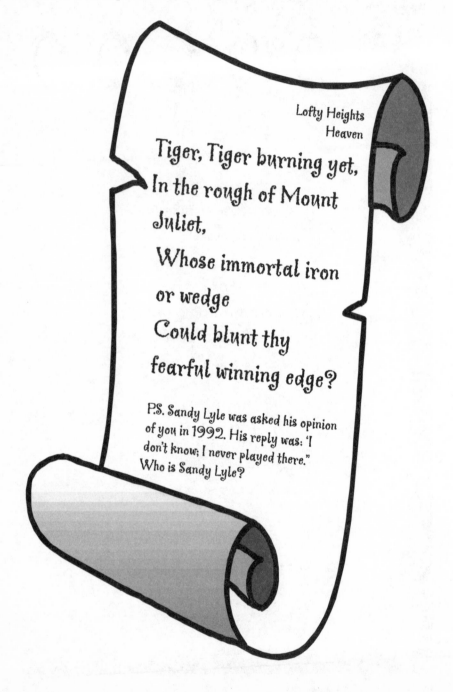

Lofty Heights
Heaven

Tiger, Tiger burning yet,
In the rough of Mount
Juliet,
Whose immortal iron
or wedge
Could blunt thy
fearful winning edge?

P.S. Sandy Lyle was asked his opinion
of you in 1992. His reply was: 'I
don't know; I never played there."
Who is Sandy Lyle?

From **Flann O'Brien**, author of *At Swim-Two-Birds*, to **Jamie O'Neill**, author of *At Swim, Two Boys*:

Mylesian Fields
Heaven

Dear Mr O'Neill,

Having placed in my mouth sufficient bread for three minutes' chewing, I withdrew my powers of sensual perception and retired into the privacy of your book. Now, the brother, as is well known, couldn't look at a bit of plagiarism without choking on his bile, be the hokey. Oh begob, he warned me right enough, above in the digs with the married sister last Sundah night. 'Flann', sez he, 'don't be bothering yourself with that looderamawn O'Neill – he'd put the heart crossways in you, and him after usin' the title of your greatest work of litherathure.'

A good book may have three openings entirely dissimilar but, bedad, this is the first time I heard of two books with (nearly) the wan title. Fair play to you, Jamie, for you set out to reinvent Dublin literature but you recognised the limitations of your artistry. Why invent your own title when you can borrow one from myself? Sure and begod, wasn't I finished with the thing altogether myself! I look forward to your next opus and, especially, the title thereof. Might I suggest The Tired Policeman?

Trusting this finds you, as it leaves me, In the pink.

Flann O'Brien

From **Jimmy O'Dea**, comic genius, to the **Enlisted Army of Irish Stand-Up Comics**:

The Green Room
Heaven

Lads,

Laugh? I thought
I'd never start!

Yours,
not amused,
Jimmy O'Dea

Nancy Mitford, doyenne of aristocratic style, codifier of the rituals of U and non-U, writes an open letter to the members of the Irish parliament:

To all members of the Dáil and Senate, greetings:

It is very unlikely that many of you know who I was. The paths of your ancestors and mine were unlikely to have crossed, unless perhaps an ancestor of mine was giving one of yours a good old-fashioned crack of a whip whilst riding past the mud cabin on the way to a lawn meet at some grand country house. I was, indeed I suppose I still am, a Mitford. My father was a Peer of the Realm, one sister married a Duke, another a Guinness (the family, of course, not the drink), another was Hitler's girlfriend. You get my drift. The paths of the aristocrat and the muck savage rarely cross. I address you this letter to you out of sheer distress.

As the arbiter of good taste and manners whilst on Earth, I was the world leader in such matters. It is patently obvious that very few of you would know the distinction between pudding and dessert, sofa and couch, lavatory and toilet, flat and apartment, not to mention the finer points of U and non-U pronunciation and dress.

A member of your Senate, on a visit to Brussels, ordered his Steak Tartare well done! Imagine the hilarity in the kitchen of that very grand restaurant when that order was delivered. Then of course there was poor Mr Killilea, MEP, who thought bon appetit was someone's name. Not to mention dear Deputy Brendan Daly who told the Lower House that a former member who had just died would be missed by all the members, especially those who had predeceased him. Well, my dears, I have heard some parliamentary howlers in my time but that must surely take the Eamon de Valera Prize for Asinine Magnificence.

I now direct my attention to the dress sense of lady members. The Deputy Prime Minister, Ms Harney, and the leader of the Senate, Mrs Mary O'Rourke, are hereby awarded my special accolade for their unfailing devotion to 'Mother of the Bride' attire. Ladies I beseech you, is there really a need to look like vegetarian lady novelists on the way to a country wedding, when all you have to do is look across Leinster Lawn to Merrion Square for inspiration? There you will find the former HQ of Miss Sybil Connolly. I have mentioned your case to Miss Connolly and she is taking a special interest in you. She says that she is willing to communicate with you through a medium – much as dear Mr Yeats did. Perhaps we might even use that dear sweet granddaughter of Mr Yeats's – now what is she called, ah yes Síle. Miss Connolly is of the opinion that you ladies could well attain the status of leaders of world fashion with only the slightest effort.

I simply cannot bring myself to write of how gentlemen members dress. I was devastated at the loss of Mr Haughey and his Charvet shirts. Such panache. Such elegance. I am most shocked at the male members choice of footwear. Mr Lobb or Mr Maxwell of Dover Street can hardly get a look in what with all that M&S high street tat. And dear, dear, dear, the slip-on shoe. Must we have the slip-on shoe? The late Queen Mother was most terribly distressed when she saw a member of her own family, Mr John Bowes Lyon, pitch up at a gentlemen's club wearing slip-ons.
So now, here is a chance for all you dashing Irish MPs to poke the Brits in the eye with a stick and show that real style rests on the other side of the mainland.
I remain, yours ever vigilant,

Nancy Mitford

Mae West, Hollywood legend, writes to RTÉ news reader
Anne Doyle:

                                    West Corner
                                    Heaven

Dear Ann (or is it Anne),

Isn't the gossip press a terrible
thing? My dear, I too have been a
victim of its poison. Now darling,
I know you like a good martini, and
I hope you stick to the vodka
because, let me tell you, gin is
bad for two things: sin and the
complexion. And remember what I say
about martinis: The martini is a
lethal drink, have one at most, two
you're under the table, three you're
under the host'.

     Sweetheart, I want to address the
question of your future. Time stands
still for no man and it sure don't
stand still for no woman either.
Time comes when every gorgeous
newsreader gets put out to grass
and a girl must have a contingency
plan in place. Look what happened
to that dear old girl who was there
before you. Can't even remember her
name.

Now you listen to your old Aunty
Mae and you won't go far wrong.
Junior Ministers are not your scene
dear. Now that you have reached the
half ton – in age I mean – it's time
for you to start thinking BIG, and I
mean BIG, dear.

You need to grab yourself a
Senior Minister or a Taoiseach (did
I spell that right? Gaelic ain't my
thing – other than the Gaelic
coffee). I reckon that the hunky
Bertie has another ten years in
office and he needs a woman like
you to keep him there.

Well, sweetie, Aunty Mae will be
watching your progress. You're
already on the RTE board of bosses,
so shift yourself and get running
the country, baby.

Your number one fan,
Mae 'Martini' West

P.S. You should be appointed to the
Senate and be known as Senator Anne
Doyle (SAD).

49

Diana, Princess of Wales, writes to businessman, polo player and socialite Oliver Caffrey:

My Royal Corner

My dear Oliver,

We so desperately need you here. Not that I am trying to hasten your demise but there's simply nobody up here who can throw a decent party like you can. The wine is chateaux-bottled muck, 'chateaux despair' I call it. One never sees even a tiny daub of caviare not to mention a white truffle or a scrap of lobster. The sort of things, darling, that we took for granted in the old days on the polo circuit. Just good old-fashioned store-cupboard fare as you would call it.

And, as for the gowns. Well I can only agree with Robert O'Byrne, on seeing that his monks habit at Glenstall was not designed by YSL 'Yuk, yuk, yuk'. However, unlike that dear modest Robert I can't hitch up my skirts and rush off to The Irish Times.

My accommodation also leaves a great deal to be desired. Do you think they have the imagination and style of an Oliver Caffrey? Not a bit of it. You my dear, would ensconce me in a fine four-poster. Up here it's a hard bench for your poor dear Diana.

I always felt we had so much in common, especially with my Irish blood. I think it was you who told me the full story of my relationship to Lord Fermoy. I hear Michael Flatley has bought a house near Fermoy. I do hope you are advising him on the interiors – at least there might be some hope of averting a disaster.

If you hear of anyone interesting coming this way would you send me up a bag of goodies? I send you and all my gorgeous Irish boys lots and lots of love.

Yours ever,

Di

From **Seán Ó Riada**, Irish composer and musician, to **Ronan Keating** and **all boy bands of Ireland**:

Tír na nÓg
Heaven

A Bhuachaillaí,

Occasionally I take a break from sitting on celestial clouds playing Irish airs on the harpsichord and tune into what the youth of Ireland are listening to on 2FM. All too often what I hear sends shivers up my spine, when my ears are assaulted by the unseemly screeches of Boy Bands who have as much music between them as a bag of Kilkenny Cats on a market day. Bleached hair and tight trousers to show off your assets are no substitute for musical talent.

Go down to West Cork and listen any Sunday to the little choir at Cuil Aodha lifting their voices in unison to praise God, charming mankind with song and melody, sweet sounds that give delight and hurt not. The man at the bar in Baile Mhuirne never said a truer word than when he looked up from his pint and remarked: 'They say that there are musical differences between the choir at Cuil Aodha and Boyzone. There are indeed. They are musical and Boyzone are different!!'

Slán - here's my cloud!

Seán Ó Riada

From **Robert Emmet,** Irish patriot and martyr, to **Niall Quinn,** footballer:

The Scaffold
Heaven

Sir,

I read with alarm and disquiet in an Irish Sunday newspaper that you thought your colleague Roy Keane's ill-tempered, foul-mouthed outburst with the Irish soccer team in Saipan was comparable to, and of as significant historic import as, my 1803 speech from the dock before I was hanged as a rebel. You also had the gall to compare it to the fine oratory and wit of Brendan Behan, the passionate rhetoric of Eamon de Valera and the heartfelt sentiments of Michael Collins.

My dear Mr Quinn, is there no end to you arrogance? Never confuse commercialism with patriotism, nor vulgar profanity and obscenity with fine words and high ideals. Do not confuse and equate the ability and skill to kick a ball around a football pitch with the moral authority to speak form the high ground.

You have disgraced yourselves again. Not until you are seen for the crass, vulgar and mindless louts that you have shown yourselves to be will you be rightly consigned to the lowest pit of Hell. There will be special torments for you there: you will have to eat your coarse and crude words and regurgitate them daily.

Only when you and your memory have been consigned to the dustbin of history, then, and not until then, let my epitaph be written.

Yours, with head held high,

Robert Emmet

53

Bertie Smyllie, editor of *The Irish Times* from 1934 to 1954, and one of the giants of Irish journalism, observes some of the developments at his old newspaper:

Hacks Corner
Heaven

Gentlemen and others,

It has always been my opinion that the best newspapers are run by committee. A committee of one. It was a view I cherished since being interned in Rühleben when I was a very young man. I imagine at this stage you are all rushing for The Times Atlas of the World to see where that place might be. All except for those few good men on the Foreign Desk and dear darling Robert O'Byrne.

Yet, of course, I err here. You have so readily abandoned your greatest asset: Mr O'Byrne is lost to you. And who are you? Fools, Catholics, lefties, vegetarians, women and women with opinions. That, sirs, is what the Old Lady of Westmoreland Street is now made up of.

The Garda Review! The Garda Review! For God's sake, it might as well have been The Irish Catholic. No great editor can ever come from that sort of tripe. I cut my teeth at the Versailles Peace Conference not at the Garda conference in Killarney.

I never for one moment thought Bertie Smyllie would find himself in agreement with a Fianna Fáil-er, but I must say, sirs, that Haughey fellow was right (wing).

For years you all sat about cursing the Major. The Major is of the old school and beyond reproach in Smyllie's book. Lunch at the Kildare Street Club. Bespoke suits, a country house, shooting with peers of the realm. That's the sort of life an Irish Times man should lead. Not pints in pubs one has never heard of.

I leave you with this thought. I swear that if a woman is ever appointed I shall return and haunt you all and pour bile on your wretched laptops.

I remain,
Your only editor,

R. M. SMYLLIE

Bertie Smyllie, on hearing that Geraldine Kennedy has been made editor of *The Irish Times*, is slightly confused but writes to congratulate her nonetheless:

Hacks Corner
Heaven

Dear Miss Kennedy,
I send you sincere congratulations on your appointment as women's editor of The Irish Times. I was always of the opinion that we needed more women's features in the paper and, now that you are in control of such matters, I feel my old paper is in a safe pair of mittens.

May I make so bold, from this distance, as to make a few suggestions which may be of some help to you in your new post. Now I am aware that my prejudices are well known in this area, but, at the risk of rattling on, could I suggest that Robert O'Byrne be brought back as assistant women's editor. He's just the boy for the job as your right-hand man.

Now you must realise that Robert is not a handbag carrier for rich ladies who lunch, so I must insist that he be taken seriously. Think of all the fun you two could have arranging for new and exciting knitting patterns, recipes, flower arranging. Robert could also be sent as a roving reporter to that much neglected guild of ladies, the Irish Countrywomen's Association.

My dear Miss Kennedy, in your hands I feel that the post of women's editor will have an entirely new edge. Now speaking of edges, you might also think of inviting Terry Keane to write a diary from her exile. She's well connected, you know, and that sort of thing is not to be sniffed at. I understand her husband is still Lord Chief Justice.

One final touch which would add flourish as you enter upon your new post might be to move that Eileen Battersby girl on. She has done a great job for culture; now perhaps it is time to give her agriculture. I feel certain that there is a role too for that Vincent Browne chappie. He could become Kevin Myers; Kevin Myers could become John Waters; John Waters could become Frank MacDonald; Frank MacDonald could become Conor Brady; Conor Brady could become Maeve Binchy and Maeve Binchy could become herself – I could go on like this forever...

God Save the King,
Yours truly,
    R. M. 'Bertie' Smyllie
  The Real Editor of The Irish Times.

P.S. Are you still a member of the PD Party (Poor Dessie Party)?

James Dillon, former leader of Fine Gael, writes to **Michael Noonan**, a more recent former leader of Fine Gael:

Revered Leaders Corner
Heaven

My dear Noonan,

Had we ever met in life I think it most unlikely that we would have sat over the finer vintages in the Shelbourne Hotel. That is perhaps a generational rather than a class thing. I was, indeed still am, a ferocious old snob. Monocle, signet ring, etc. – the symbols, dear boy, the symbols. The cut of a man's jib, often, though not always, defines who he is. I do after all spring from John Blake Dillon's family. We were gentry, you know. So were the Dockrell's and the Cosgraves. Horses, hounds, houses.

Be that as it may, I turn, as I invariably do, to serious and not to sartorial matters; to matters of bread and butter and not of mere bloodlines and breeding. This leadership business is quite beyond me. Fine Gael has now had more leaders than the bands which march down O'Connell Street on Saint Patrick's Day.

I am fond of the maxims of Edmund Burke. He said all it requires for evil to prosper is for good men to do nothing. Now look here, you are a young man. If I am not mistaken, the Dáil record registers you as a man of classical learning and most certainly of wit. Spartacus and the slave war will not be unknown to you as an actual historical event. I suggest you take it as your moniker and rise up against the forces of mediocrity in Fine Gael. There is no reason why a clever backbench revolt – led by Gay Mitchell (tell Jim Mitchell to stay at home) – should not see you restored to your rightful place, when Bertie and the fools who follow him have finally driven the economy back into recession. The best place to lead this revolt from is the private bar at Lillie's. I knew it as Jammet's in the old days. Jolly good oysters and claret.

But I digress. The reason I suggest Lillie's is because there is a very interesting group of influential young bloods patronising it in the late evenings. You would be a sort of Oswald Mosley to them. They are eager for leadership and all from terribly decent Fine Gael families – mostly Jesuit boys, so just say you went to Clongowes, they won't know you didn't, as some of them are cocained out of their brains and incapable of reading the old boys register or clever enough to look it up.

Carpe diem, grab the day, dear boy. No point hanging about in miserable old Limerick. This could be the greatest come back since Lazarus. Look to it!

Yours very truly,

JAMES DILLON

P.S. Ring Maurice Manning and tell him his brilliant biography of me is still No. 1 in Heaven.

Seán Lemass, former Taoiseach, writes to **Bertie Ahern** with a few words of friendly advice:

Dear Bertie,

You may or may not know that I was the only man alive who was feared by Charlie Haughey. I once told him to get his hair cut and he left for the barbers immediately. It must strike you, therefore, that a word of advice from me might be worth listening to. You know my old saying 'a rising tide lifts all boats'? Well the tide has been rising in your favour for some time now, which is why I'm writing to you: for the cautionary times that might lie ahead.

Now, Bertie, you know what Charlie said of you. It was something about you being the cutest, the most cunning, etc., etc. Now coming from that cute hoor there must be more than a little substance to it. I've seen you in action and I know his judgement was not misplaced.

Bacon – the philosopher I mean and not the stuff sold by Ned O'Keeffe – once said that 'nothing does more damage in a State than when cunning men pass for wise'. So it is here that I expect you to show a little wisdom. You weathered the battle with the Cardinal beautifully. Well played. It could have brought down a lesser man. I was never one for those old priests myself. Didn't I stand by and watch Dev licking their holy arses and holding Ireland back 100 years in the process?

But here I come to my point. I have watched that Miss Larkin – the woman you're living with. Why don't you make an honest woman of her? What in heaven's name is stopping you? Didn't we pass the bloody divorce legislation. Remember Dolly Parton.

The final thing you need to be thinking about is watching your back. A Fianna Fáil leader is never more in danger than when he thinks he's safe (remember your friend Jack Lynch). I can tell you there are bogmen there on those back benches who have BIFFO's knives sharpened (for your back).

Well, all that Tribunal lark has us all in stitches up here. Sure didn't they try to screw me with that sort of tripe as well. But like myself, Bertie, 'tis only the power that interests you not the money. Keep it that way and by the time you retire the directorships will be flowing in to you.

One last word of caution. Watch that Michael McDowell fella like a hawk. He'd have you in trouble now quicker that the Harney one. We don't want another Harry Whelehan situation, but at least you're not a God-help-us like that poor auld Albert Reynolds. 'Keep 'em sweatin'' was his philosophy when he had the dance halls. Well he kept us sweatin' as well because we never knew where the next passport was going. It's a wonder he didn't have Idi Amin investing in Ireland and in Longford. I suppose Osma bin Laden got a passport from Bourke and that's why he can't be found.

Enough for now. I'll write to you again before the next election.

Your former Taoiseach and leader,

Seán Lemass

P.S. The world will end by a massive "Flood" in March 2003. The Flood Tribunal will come to a premature and final end. Ring Dunlop and tell him to hold fire.

W. T. Cosgrave, founding father of the State, writes to the West's most famous TD, **Michael Ring** of Mayo:

Dear Mr Ring,

There can be no doubt in my mind about it, but not since the time of Daniel O'Connell has a political genius of your calibre emerged in Ireland. You come from that great tradition born of the West of Ireland, a son of that very soil that gave us our finest Irish blood.

I have watched your progress since you won that first by-election and returned to Fine Gael the confidence it was lacking. You have all the qualities of a great leader. You are modest. You are without vanity of any kind. You are as fine an orator as Cicero himself. You have balls of steel. You are an auctioneer. Your are from the West. Your have no truck with Dublin jackeens. You have told Bertie Ahern where to get off. You have told half of Dáil Éireann where to get off. You are a man's man.

I'm gettin' carried away. Sure if you were any better 'tis up for Pope I'd be puttin' you instead of just the mere leadership of poor Fine Gael.

Keep up the good work and watch your back with that Enda Kenny fella. He comes from a long tradition of cute hoors and he speaks fluent French. Never trust a Mayoman who speaks fluent French. Remember the Year of the French. The French are on the sea said the Sean bhean bhocht.

Slán agus beannacht,

W. T. Cosgrave

Mary MacSwiney, 1872–1942, republican activist, writes to **Pádraig Flynn,** former EU commissioner and another former friend of CJH:

The Republican Plot
Heaven

Dear Pee,

I supported de Valera until his decision to enter the Dáil and recognise the legitimacy of the Free State, so I'm well placed to give you a lash of my tongue. 'The Messiah from Mayo' you once called yourself. Well, I can tell you 'tis more 'The Mucker from Mayo' that would fit more comfortably on your dunder head.

Well, if it wasn't enough for you to loose the presidential election on poor Brian Lenihan in favour of that Robinson one. Then you make a complete eejit of yourself on The Late Late with yer man Gay Byrne. Sure, you could never teach a yob to keep his gob shut. And if that wasn't enough you had to go on about all your feckin' houses and how you got the roads for the West of Ireland. I suppose you were out there in Europe ordering your steak tartare 'well done'. Just as well you had the pioneer pin or you would be drinking Blue Tower and Black Nun lest the mercy of the most divine saviour.

'Tis a great consolation to all right-thinking people that you produced such a brilliant political dynasty in Mayo. 'Beverly', said Paddy Lindsay, 'What a common Mayo name.' 'Beverly Cooper Flynn' – is there a hyphen or a hymen? Is that a rock band? What a pity you didn't call her Alice Cooper Flynn and she might have dragged in the youth vote.

I would be careful buy who I'd buy an insurance policy, a coffin or an offshore investment from . That poor Charlie Bird was worn to a thread after all them High Court actions and he a good God-fearing product of the RTÉ newsroom, the very font of all Irish wisdom, justice and truth. If you had any sense now you'd become a tax exile somewhere exotic like Innis Boffin. That way the wimmin of Ireland would be rid of yer beautiful mug and the auld dyed hair.

Good luck now Pee
Up Mná na hÉireann,

Mary MacSwiney

From the deceased **judges** at the **Nuremberg Trials** to the **chairmen of all Irish Tribunals** present and future:

Judicial Corner
Heaven

To all whom it may concern, greetings:

Chekhov tells us that the most intolerable people are provincial celebrities. There is also an old Bosnian proverb which goes 'who lies for you will lie against you'. Here we feel is the very kernel of what your excellencies face as you attempt to unravel the weighty fabric of truth and half-truth which assails your ears and confronts your senses each day.

Let us take first the case of Mr Lawlor: He is perhaps the greatest example in recent history of habit breeding chaos where it should have bred order. We thought the most suitable long-term punishent for Mr Lawlor would be to set him the task of writing a new version of The Decay of Lying. The great mass of people, Hitler said, will more easily fall victim to a big lie than to a small one. Now do you see that Mr Lawlor and the great dictator have more than a little in common.

Your first victim is also living proof that no man lies more effectively than the man who is indignant. But will savage indignation cause the heart of Mr Lawlor to be rent asunder? Maybe he should be sent to ghost the autobiography of Malcolm McArthur.. But we think that is being a little unfair to Mr McArthur.

Now to Mr Haughey: He believes politics to be not a bad profession, that is, if you succeed in it. If you fail, you have two options: You can put your little paw out to a shopkeeper and take a brown envelope or you can write a book. Having chosen the former course Mr Haughey has received sufficient punishment and, like that General whose name escapes us, having looked upon his injuries he knew it was not necessary to die. One voice, one leader, as Mr Mara would have it.

We attest finally that not one judge at Nuremberg was a member of the Fianna Fáil Party.

The Justices

From the **deceased directors** of Ede and Ravenscroft, wig-makers, who write out of genuine concern to deputy **Donie Cassidy**, newly elected member of Dáil Éireann (forever):

Wax Corner
Heaven

Dear Deputy Cassidy,

We beg that you may forgive our impertinence in writing to you on so delicate a matter, given that we have the Royal seal of approval and that you are an Irish republican. We are, however, the world's most distinguished wig-makers and our clients include the Lord Chief Justice and every barrister of note in England and Ireland. We do not manufacture what are nowadays called rugs or crown toppers but proper ceremonial wigs, which are worn on important and grand occasions of state.

You are a man with a sense of dignity and style. You are also in possession of the finest head of hair in the Irish parliament. It is, therefore, that we write in the earnest hope that you could persuade Miss Celia Larkin to use her good offices with the Prime Minister, Mr Ahern, to reinstate the use of wigs in the Irish parliament on ceremonial occasions. We are aware that Her Majesty the Queen will visit Ireland in the very near future and we thought, when she visits the Dáil and Senate, it would be very grand indeed for Mr Speaker in the Dáil and the Speaker in the Senate to be wearing full-bottom wigs.

We also thought the Dáil ushers could be put into wigs. I'm sure this idea would be met with great joy, as their union would insist on a pay increase for those poor dear polite boys. They would also have to get a powder allowance. No, Mr Cassidy, not cocaine, but white powder for their wigs.

If you facilitated this request, you would become a national hero and, if we may say so, we could be in a position to ask Her Majesty to do a little something for you. We think Sir Donie has a very nice ring to it; or what about Lord Cassidy of Castlepollard?

We beg to remain your humble and obedient servants,

The deceased directors of
Ede and Ravenscroft
(Wig-makers by Appointment)

Des Traynor, accountant to Charles Haughey, definitely died in 1994. He became the fall guy for many of the explanations sought from Mr Haughey during the McCracken Tribunal. This 'dead man strategy' has become a notorious part of Irish political farce. Here Traynor writes to his old client:

Bagmans Corner
Heaven

Dear Charlie,

Who would doubt you? Certainly not I. What an inspired idea. Not even my own creative accounting could have dreamt it up. 'The Dead Man Strategy'. Such a great stroke old pal! It leaves even the Tallaght Strategy standing. Sure even GUBU, the Arms Trial and 'an Irish solution to an Irish problem' pale into insignificance beside that one.

I suppose the Irish people in their wisdom will forgive you. It certainly looked as if the people of Kerry didn't care much for 'tribunals' when you launched the Dingle Regatta recently. I was wondering if that was a Charvet shirt you were wearing. How many did you buy in the end? I hear there is a man in the States who buys a new one every day and burns the old ones.

I suppose you gave the old ones to Terry Keane for her favourite charity – herself.

I always told you that she would cause you problems. It was alright for Parnell to be "liaising" with an English woman but not you. You should have had one of those news readers from RTÉ, and I don't mean Aengus Mac Grionna but one of those beautiful show stoppers with the dyed hair. Much more your style.

How is poor Maureen coping? Do you remember the day the Arab sheikh was coming to Kinsealy and Maureen was still in the hall with the hoover. A great girl with Ireland's best interests at heart – just like old Seán Lemass. He's fairly furious with you, but at times we sit and joke about what a clever old hoor you are.

I wonder if that new Minister for Justice might try to screw you. With his Blue Shirt background you'd never know. Anyway, old pal, I'd say it will be some time before we see you up here. So keep the pecker up and keep away from those 'big fellas' with the big cheques – cash only (like the church collection – no records).

Your old bagman and friend,

Des

P.S. Ask Judge Flood would he like to visit me on a one-way ticket. Heaven is like FF – once inside, you are inside forever; leave once (like Harney) and you are out forever.

Sir **Roger Casement**, Irish patriot, writes to **Brendan Howlin**, TD, member of the Labour Party:

Dear Brendan,

Ireland is rearing them yet! The English destroyed me by accusing me of the English vice, and now our own people are trying to do the same to you!

But what on Earth are you trying to achieve by denying it, before the accusation has been made? You are almost as bad as my near contemporary, Oscar Wilde! Remember what terrible destruction he brought upon himself by lashing out at the boorish Marquis of Queensbury! All polite society quite detested Queensbury but, in the end, it was Wilde who was picking oakum for two years.

After all my travels abroad, there was one thing that struck me about the Irish people: the more a man denies a thing, the more the Irish believe that thing to be true. 'No smoke without fire', and all that. There is no other race on God's Earth who so thoroughly disbelieve a denial.

Brendan, cease this premature denial! There is a time and a place for Swift's savage indignation, but this is not the time and this is not the place. Follow my example and exhibit a lofty disdain to such accusations, if and when they come.

After all, apparently it is no longer a crime to have such inclinations in Ireland. Always remember that when they accuse you of screaming remind them you are a-howlin'.

Yours ever,

Roger Casement

P.S. You have failed again to become leader of the Labour Party. You should resign from the party and join Fine Gael – they change leaders regularly – it is your only chance to be Taoiseach. Failed leaders do not make it in Heaven.

Jonathan **Swift** and **W. S. Gilbert** give vent to their spleen as they pen a new satire on the Irish nation called:

Eire go Breá Corner
Heaven

The State of Ireland

Ireland has forsaken all her wicked courses
Which empties the Dáil benches and creates new divorces.
Her respect is reserved for higher rank and splendour,
For the greater his position the bigger the offender.
Not a TD, Senator or builder bearing CIE bus passes
Has no respect from the Upper Middle Classes.
Every shady dog-food maker, whatever his rank
Commands the largest loans from the Anglo-Irish Bank.

Dublin is now beautiful – we've done it willy-nilly,
With the help of Johnny Ronan, and his navvies from Piccadilly.
We have solved the labour shortage, by importing all the colours
But Mary Harney fears the possibilities of Mullahs.
We have purged our native land of all discrimination
Begorrah is abolished in favour of titillation.
No social trash is welcome unless its custom made
And McAleese checks it for the Paddy's Day Parade.

Our Peerage we've reinstated on a completely different basis:
Charlie Haughey is a Duke giving cups at Galway Races,
The Guinnesses and Gormanstons no longer seek admission
For gentlemen of class get no proper recognition.
Who knows we may soon count in the ranks of our Debretts
The TD fresh from jail saying 'I have no known regrets'.
Lord Lawlor and Viscount Lowry we shall embrace so very sweetly
And then poor auld Ireland will be truly fecked completely.

Oliver J. Flanagan, former Fine Gael TD, Knight of St Gregory and staunch supporter of all just causes, writes to the Minster for Foreign Affairs, Brian Cowen, offering some avuncular advice:

Holy Joe's Corner
Heaven

Dear Cowen,

BIFFOs they call us Laois-Offaly men; or is it just Offaly men who get that appellation? Sure wasn't Lord Offaly the subsidiary title of the Duke of Leinster and wasn't he the most powerful man in Ireland - almost as powerful as you are now. You belong to that party of national salvation, but sure aren't you a neighbour's child and your auld fella Ber wasn't a bad auld skin.

Here's a bit of advice from one cute hoor to another. Don't sit on your laurels now that you have secured a victory in the Nice referendum. That other cute hoor Bertie will now be trying to consolidate his position and take the credit for your hard work, even though PJ Mara had done all the spade work for nothing. This, of course, saved PJ from the bother of wondering and remembering where to lodge the money. Strike while the iron is hot. Take that Conor Lenihan fella out to lunch and fill him full of drink. (I can't undertand why Bertie didn't make him Minister for Finance.) He's just the boy to stir up the back benches. Get him to go in at Taoiseach's Question Time drunk to the gills and breathing fury from the back benches. You could also get Ned O'Keeffe well oiled, and sure between the pair of them they could have you elected Taoiseach in a week.

Now to more pressing matters. As you know Fianna Fáil is perceived to be very pro the Palestinian cause. Now let me tell you that is a very bad move. You'd want to put a gag on Mick Lanigan and all the other Arab lovers in the party as soon as you become Taoiseach. I can tell you boy, stick with them auld Jews and you won't need any brown envelopes. Sure aren't they running America? Personally, I've not much time for them, as is well known from my remarks in the Dáil after the last war, but they won't do you any harm.
Go on ya boy ya.

Best wishes,

Oliver J.

P.S. I see that my son Charles and your hero Charlie Haughey have on thing in common: both are ex TDs.

Jack Lynch writes from Heaven to his old adversary Charles Haughey:

Dear Charlie,

Christy Ring – a man rarely given to small talk – button-holed me the very day I arrived here and asked: 'How did you feel about Charlie Haughey attending your funeral in Cork?' I had just been listening to Francis Stuart, explaining in the most tongue-in-cheek manner to Saint Peter, why he supported the Nazis during the Second World War. Stuart said he always had 'a soft spot for the underdog'. You could have knocked me down with a feather until I realised the man was joking. I don't think Peter quite got it, though.

I too, Charlie, have always had a soft spot for the underdog. God knows (how odd that expression seems up here) there can be few in Ireland at this time to whom that term applies with more relevance than yourself.

A source close to the throne here had a great laugh when he looked down and saw you arriving at my funeral. Even here we are not safe from bitchiness. He turned to me and said, 'Do you know what that fellow Haughey said you were suffering from when your illness was first announced in the media?' 'I suppose he said amnesia,' said I. 'No,' said yer man, 'he said you had AIDS.' Even I saw the humour in that one.

But, be that as it may, Ring got me thinking of the old days and of how wiley a divil you were, indeed, still are. I looked at all those faces at my funeral – looking like the Shroud of Turin – and suddenly there you were shaking hands with Des O'Malley, and I thought to myself, 'Fair play to the auld rascal, hasn't he got balls of brass,' as Frank Dunlop might say.

And do you know Charlie at that moment I forgave you every sin and transgression. There was talk of nothing else up here for weeks after. Dev, an ardent fan of yours, could hardly contain himself. I suppose he's right. Then he always was, as you well know!

So there we have it, Charlie, your old adversary forgives you all. Sure after that, tribunals and the rest are just plain sailing. Speaking of which I see you still have the 'Celtic Mist'.

Good luck now, and keep your sliotar dry and your Charvet shirts well laundered.

Slán agus beannacht,

Jack

P.S. Please Charlie, write to me and forgive me for my role in the Arms Crisis. You were found not guilty, which means you were not involved (in anything). Kevin Boland always said that you were innocent. Blaney said that I should have been shot. They are both up here still hoping for a United Ireland – hope springs eternal.

Eoin MacNeill, republican, Celtic scholar and grandfather of the Minister for Justice, **Michael McDowell**, writes to his grandson with some sound political advice:

The Nationalist Plot
Heaven

Micheál a stóir,

I began life as a humble court clerk. You can imagine, therefore, the not inconsiderable pride I felt when you assumed the office of Attorney General. I need hardly tell you that your further elevation to the office of Minister for Justice has left me in a tailspin of delight.

Do you know I was recently accused of pride and arrogance in taking pleasure in the advancement of my own family! Can you imagine anyone ever associating any of those sins with our family? A more humble self-effacing lot could hardly ever have walked God's Earth.

Your fortitude in the face of adversity has been a great joy to me. Didn't I lose my seat myself in 1927, after they tried to damn me with the report of the Boundary Commission which determined the Northern Ireland border. By the way, you're not doing enough to defend my name on that matter. Tell them Eoin MacNeill had no truck with boundary divisions, and anyway didn't I resign before the report was published? Always a good one to remember that if your back is against the wall: resign before the report comes out.

But I digress. Now that you are Minister for Justice I want a little favour. Doesn't everyone says you! You know I countermanded the order for the Easter Rising given by Pearse and the other old fairies around him. I've had very bad press over that and I'd like something done about it. Can you imagine someone of the lower orders like the new Labour leader Pat Rabbitte standing up in the Dáil and accusing your grandfather of wrong-footing during a crucial moment of Irish history. How dare they? I AM IRISH HISTORY.

What could I do? How could I rely on Pearse and all the other fairies in kilts to run a rebellion. Someone had to cry halt. I told Pearse the other day, when I saw him prancing around up here in a big green dress by Sybil Connolly with a big golden harp from Claddagh Records, that you will have your revenge on the Irish fairies. Why don't you reverse all that liberal legislation brought in by Maire Geoghan-Quinn? That would be a poke in the eye for the green fairy brigade.

I know I can trust you on these matters. Sure didn't you deliver the greatest bon mot in Irish parliamentary history when, speaking of the two Mitchell brothers, you described Gay as 'the lesser of two evils'.

Is mise le mease mór agus gach dea ghui,

Grandpapa

Erskine Childers, father of Erskine Hamilton Childers and author of *The Riddle of the Sands*, writes an open letter from Heaven to the **Members of Dáil** and **Seanad Éireann**:

Ladies and Gentlemen (I use the term loosely),

One of the great benefits of an English public school education is the natural sense of superiority and belief in self that it visits upon one at a tender age. At the end of my life it did me little good as I was slaughtered by a bunch of common Free State peasants. Being a gentleman, I asked my son to shake hands with my executioners.

All that is very well in retrospect, but it does not save me from my nightly exposure in this life to a large dose of you lot on Oireachtas Report. God help the poor people saddled with the task of putting that rubbish together and making sense of the inarticulate, incoherent offerings made in that hallowed chamber by the greatest collection of angels ever assembled in the name of Ireland.

You may recall that when de Valera called James Dillon a 'West Brit', Dillon retorted with the famous quip: 'Mr de Valera, my family was fighting for Irish freedom when your family was banging bongos on the back streets of

Barcelona.' How very little has changed.

The best howler of recent years was made by Deputy Brendan Daly of Clare when speaking of the death of an old, long-forgotten TD. He informed the House that the deputy would be sorely missed, especially by the members who had predeceased him! Such great oratory.

John B. Keane once said: 'Take the ball on the hop and a hop to the Dáil.' But really most of you would be better served by never opening your mouths. Can't somebody take that Ned O'Keeffe aside and suggest that he request bilingual subtitles for his invaluable contributions. Perhaps he could share the cost with Mr Healy-Rae. Also perhaps Donie Cassidy could recommend a wig-maker to Mr Healy-Rae.

There are times listening to you all when I feel that it was not worth dying for Ireland.

I remain ladies and gentlemen (in the loosest possible sense),

Yours truly,

Erskine Childers

Mother Teresa of Calcutta writes to **Mary O'Rourke**, Mother of the Senate and Mother of the Nation:

Bathtub Corner
Heaven

Hail Mary,

Mother Mary O'Rourke those rotters in the Press Gallery used to call you. I suppose they still do. I'm from Albania and you're from Athlone so I suppose we have a lot in common coming from two cesspits. Anyway you are a saint and I am a saint. You, too, are a reverend mother, but I never listened to Morning Ireland in the bath as I'm more of a Radio 4 girl myself. I suppose it's the influence of the British Raj in India.

I'm surprised you weren't more influenced by the British Raj in Ireland. They're not the worst, though I know you're a rampant republican like poor Mr Haughey and your dear late brother, who speaks so highly of you up here. You must be terribly proud of the two nephews, Brian and the other

fellow Connor. Tell that Connor fella to keep a
tight reign on his tongue and tell Brian Junior
to resign unless Bertie promotes him in the
next two years. You see, if he hadn't gone to
Trinity and Cambridge, he'd have got a
cabinet post. Fianna Fáil does not trust
old imperial institutions.

But sure you're an institution yourself.
I will have great gas watching you
being Reverend Mother in the Senate. It
was terribly kind of you to give me the
rosary beads when I got the freedom of
Dublin. I have them worn out up here
praying for you. I suppose you won't
contest the party leadership again.
How many votes did you get – six I
think, wasn't it? Well sure our Lord
fell three times so there's hope for
us all.

God bless you Mother O'Rourke.
Yours with all blessings,

Mother Teresa

Former minister **Noel Browne**, political radical and keeper of the conscience of the Left in Ireland, writes to offer comfort to **Ruairí Quinn**, former leader of the Labour Party:

Mother and Child Corner
Heaven

Dear Ruairí,

Few would dispute the fact that you are a decent man. Not even your enemies, if you ever had any, would question that. It was obvious when you supported Bertie and Celia when they got a belt of the Cardinal's crozier over the Dublin Castle party. Good for you. It's about time someone else in the Labour Party stood up to the Church apart from myself. Most Irishmen are hen-pecked but the whole country is priest-whipped.

What a relief it is for me to see that some of the old priests are now being revealed for what they are. Even McQuaid had been called a paedo in John Cooney's book. God, how I wished I had lived to see that. That book is banned in Heaven but John sent me up a copy.

I digress. You left the Labour Party in very poor shape. Your intentions, as always, were good and honourable. However, that is never enough. Absorbing all those former so-called republican socialists into the party was a terrible error. Now they have taken over and persuaded Finlay to come back.

The Stagg affair was a hoot. At least old Spring stood by him. I would have shafted him. Imagine getting caught in the Phoenix Park? What's that old Nazi song? 'The stag in the forest has lifted his leg and pissed all over my shoe.'

Anyway Ruairi, I wish you well, as do Brendan Corish and William Norton, both up here waiting for you. The best thing for the party would be to have Spring as lifetime dictator. It could also be a very good thing for the country (and it would stop Rabbitte's photograph appearing on every restaurant menu, with customers ordering a well-done Rabbitte).

And finally never have a woman as leader of the Labour Party. Could you imagine the jokes?

All good wishes,
Noel Browne

P.S. I heard that Lizzy McManus is the Deputy Leader of the party – I demand a recount.

Adolf Hitler writes from Hell to **Noel O'Flynn**, the Cork TD with strong opinions on refugees:

Tyrants Corner
Hell

Dear Mr O'Flynn,

How I wish I had you on my team in those final days of the final solution. You sound like a man who can get things done. You also look the part. You remind me in appearance of my old friend Göbbels. You certainly would have filled your uniform well.

I like a man with balls. Corkmen have lots of balls. How right you are to speak out on behalf of the good people of Cork. Do you want those beautiful Leeside women mingling with all those foreigners?

Take no notice of all those wet liberals. Why don't you propose the concentration camp solution for them?

There's plenty of space on the Western Road in Cork City and you could charge people in to have a look. Now that a politician can't get a brown envelope he has to look to other ways of turning a few bob.

The people of Cork would support you, apart from the pinkos and lefties who could also be rounded up. This is a decisive moment for Cork. Get your uniform made. You could be more impressive than O'Duffy. Have the shirt made in emerald green and get the Buttera band out on the streets leading the parades. O'Flynn for Führer, that's what Adolf Hitler says.

Heil O'Flynn, Heil Hitler!
Yours ever,

Adolf Hitler

Sir Paget Bourke, former British judge, and uncle of Mary Robinson, writes to the former President of Ireland:

My dear Mary,

As a Bourke of Ballina you were born to rule. As you know my own philosophy was always Rule Britannia, but one can't say that sort of thing these days. Even in the other world there is such an anti-imperial feeling. I blame that Tony Blair chap. What a common little man. In my day he would have been a minor colonial official in some backwater in India. How can he possibly have become PM?

But at least you, my dear, became President and then leader of the world. Surely there can be no stopping you now. I have come up with a very good scheme. As you are well aware, Her Majesty the Queen is making a state visit to Ireland very soon. You have met her at the Palace, as indeed I did myself when she knighted me for services to Empire in 1957. What I am suggesting is that in advance of the visit you should arrange a private audience with her and make the following proposition (now this is not as far-fetched as it may seem so do bear with me): Tell Her Majesty that you can secure a loyal section of the Irish army who are fed up with that Ahern man and the way things have gone since independence. Offer her the return of the republic and the loyalty of the army on condition that you be made Viceroy and are given complete control of the country.

What will swing it is the ban on fox-hunting in England. All the better classes will want to decamp to Ireland anyway, so you will have the complete House of Peers to choose from for your Privy Council.

It is no more than is your due as a Bourke of Ballina. You were born to rule, not to answer to common little politicians and small-minded commoners. How did you ever shake all those hands, my dear?

The other great advantage is your husband Nicholas. He looks the royal part. Oh my dear girl, just think of the opportunities. Dublin Castle as your base. Leinster House as your town house. The old parliament in College Green as your court – Nick can do all the decorating and cooking.

Do make an old man happy. You can be sure the Queen will give you a good hearing. She may want to move over herself: Fine Gael might offer her the 26 counties back when she's here, anyway. So strike while the iron is hot. They might even offer her the party – then you could become President of Fine Gaol.

God save the Queen.
Your ever loving uncle,

Paget

Lord Haw Haw writes to the much-loved and popular Lyric FM broadcaster, **Niall Carroll**:

Nazi Broadcasters Corner
Hell

Dear Mr Carroll,

Your tender youth may prevent you from knowing who I am. I, too, was once a famous broadcaster. You will recall, or perhaps not recall but have heard of, the war of 1939—45. Your history books may have referred to it as 'The Emergency' but don't be fooled by that nonsense. That was all de Valera's doing.

During that war I broadcast from Germany. 'German calling, Germany calling,' I would rattle out over the airwaves. And bloody good I was too at giving the old propaganda a good spin. Many's the Irishman alive today whose only knowledge of the war was through my brilliant machine.

There is always the need for such men in the world of broadcasting and I do feel that you are such a man, Mr Carroll. There you are on Lyric for hours on end. Then you switch on Radio 1 and you're doing an advertisement or reading the news. Turn over to RTÉ1 and there you are again beaming out at us reading some important news item at one in the morning. Such is your dedication that, if I came to Earth, I'd expect you to be making the tea in the RTÉ canteen. But great men are made from that sort of commitment.

What I am proposing Mr Carroll is that you follow my path — the path of propaganda. The world needs men such as you now. My suggestion is that you approach Saddam Hussein to be made head of propaganda for the war on the West. I can see you in Baghdad getting all the exclusives with the Arab leaders. Carroll talks to Bin Laden, Carroll goes face-to-face with Bin Laden's men. I think you get the picture.

As I saw the future with Germany, you must look to the Arab world for our salvation. Because, mark my words, one of these days we'll all be on our knees with our arses in the air facing Mecca not Decca. So get out there, you're the man to lead the van. And think about it: you could do everything, including the weather. It would be the greatest one-man show on Earth.

Grab the moment. Take the mic on the hop and a hop to Baghdad.

In the utmost haste and sincerity,
I remain sir,
Your number one fan,

Lord Haw Haw

Eamon de Valera, who needs no introduction to any audience, writes to his granddaughter **Síle**, former Minister for Arts, Heritage, Gaeltacht and the Islands and now demoted to Junior Minister for Something or Other:

Most Magnificent and Omnipotent Leaders Corner
Heaven

A stoirín mo chroí,

'Tis yourself that has the heart of your poor auld grandfather broken. I'm worn out from walking the crossroads up here pondering on where I could have gone wrong. Don't take it to heart my peteen but you know 'tis the old Chief that has only your good in mind. After all didn't I die for Ireland? My only regret was that I didn't have another life to give up.

Anyway, to the point. What ails you at all, a stoirín? You should be leader of the Party by now. What do you think I founded it for? Is it for others to be gadding about? Did you learn nothing from me, and you a slip of a girl running around the Áras swinging out of the bust of Douglas Hyde? You certainly didn't learn the céad teanga naisiúnta (first national language to you, dear). My heart does be flitters when I think of you as Minister for the Gaeltacht and you addressing the Dáil – my Dáil – in the teanga of the Sasanach. At least that cousin of yours has made a go it of but there's the touch of the Bruree cute hoor about him, despite his attitude to the Nice Treaty.

While I'm on that subject. Would you for the love of God stop talking about Boston over Berlin. Don't be following the lead of that Harney one. Sure she has no pedigree, unlike yourself – a Dev, a Dev, a Dev, a Dev for the love of God, girl. You bear the blessed name of de Valera. Not even that West Brit hoor James Dillon could take that from us.

And another thing: When Lemass said RTÉ was 'an arm of government', he didn't mean it literally, pet. Trying to break their arm was not a good idea. – even Rambo didn't go that far.

Make the best of the new job (what are you doing anyway?) and don't let it be long until you challenge that Ahern fellow. Make a big republican speech like you did in Fermoy all those years ago and that will get the boys in the back benches sitting up.

One final thing: never marry beneath you 'cause they'll soon be on top of you.

Le gach dea ghuí,

Do sheanathair dílis agus Chief

Letter from **James Boswell**, biographer of Samuel Johnson, to **Eamon Dunphy**, author, broadcaster and soccer pundit:

The Library
Heaven

Dear Eamon,

I have read your ghosted book on your hero, Roy Keane. It is indeed an onerous task to chronicle the life of the famous and the great, as I discovered when I wrote the life of the great Dr Johnson.

In setting out the life of your hero you must try to show him as Cromwell said, 'warts and all'. You, however, gave us a portrait of your hero elevated on a funeral pyre of the bodies of his former friends and sporting colleagues. You allow him to raise himself up as a hero for our times at the expense of others.

John Donne said memorably that no man is an island. You collude in the creation of Caliban isolated on an island in a backwater of arrogance, self pity and sadness. The tide has turned and your hero lies washed up on the shore.

J. B.

Lord Beaverbrook, newspaper baron and colossus of the British newspaper establishment, writes, in verse, to advise **Aengus Fanning**, of the *Sunday Independent*:

Magnates Corner
Heaven

My dear Fanning,

The role of a great newspaperman
Is to keep control while he can
Of his bolshie old staff
Oft in need of a slap
Or a P45 without jam.

You invented the great gossip Queen
And she left when she didn't become Queen
To the poor Sunday Times
Who paid her in dimes
And she still didn't become too serene.

Very sincerely yours,

Beaverbrook

P.S. Aengus, you are making a lot of money for Sir Anthony O'Reilly. I hope he appreciates your genius both as an editor and jazz player.

St Teresa of Ávila, one of the Church's great 'thinking' female saints, writes a postcard to **Dana**, MEP:

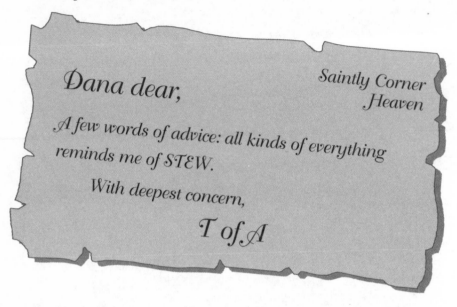

Dana dear,

Saintly Corner
Heaven

A few words of advice: all kinds of everything reminds me of STEW.

With deepest concern,

T of A

Din Joe, star of the RTÉ wireless days and the first man to present Irish dancing on the wireless (yes, you read that right, dancing on the wireless), writes to **Michael Flatley**, in the style in which only Din Joe could. Readers who can break the code are invited to write to the Managing Director of Blackwater Press; all wining entries will be passed on to a higher place where they will be set against indulgences in the next life:

BROADCASTERS CORNER
HEAVEN

DEAR MICHAEL,

TAP TAP – TAP TAP TAP TAP – TAP TAP TAP TAP TAP TAP TAP TAP – TAP TAP TAP TAP TAP TAP – TAP TAP TAP TAP TAP TAP TAP TAP. (REPEAT TO YOUR FEET'S CONTENT OR UNTIL YOU COLLAPSE.)

ALL THE BEST AND KEEP 'EM SWEATIN'.

DIN JOE

Aristotle Onassis, multimillionaire ship owner and husband of Jackie Kennedy Onassis, writes in verse to Irish businessman **Michael Smurfitt** on the virtues of one of Mr Smurfitt's favourite wines, Château Petrus, which can cost more than STG£1,000 per bottle:

Rich and Naughty Corner
Heaven

Michael,

They say that Château Petroooos
Goes frightfully well with roast goose
And at a grand a bottle
One can drink it full throttle
And pretend that one's morals ain't loose.

Regards,

Ari

P.S. I believe you own the K-Club. Are
you aware that one of its previous owners
was shot dead and still hasn't arrived in
Heaven?

Onassis also remembers Irish communications giant **Denis O'Brien**:

Rich and Naughty Corner
Heaven

Denis,

Denis, Denis, ever so bright,
Will the begrudgers ever be out of sight?
When you die your friends will say
Denis O'Brien you succeeded your way.

Regards,

Ari

P.S. If for tax reasons you don't live in
Ireland in this world, where do you
expect to live in the next world? Give me
a ring — I know you have a mobile
phone.

John Charles McQuaid, former Archbishop of Dublin, writes to his controversial biographer, journalist **John Cooney**. His Lordship's tone is uncharacteristically forgiving, if not indeed confessional:

Dear Mr Cooney,

'To err is human to forgive divine.' Absit invidia – let there be not ill-will, my dear son. We have between us, after all, as Lytton Strachey might put it, only the barrier of a common purpose. When on Earth, I, like you, had one primary function: that of arbiter between Church and State – ad majoren Dei gloriam – though I suspect, dear child, you are not a Jesuit boy yourself.

Be that as it may. You do it with the pen, I did it with a belt of the crozier. I am sure you had me in mind when you called your great book The Crozier and the Dáil. Which brings me to your other great book – your biography of me. Pay no heed to spoiled priests, the nay-sayers, the begrudgers. There is no arguing about tastes, as so many great Churchmen before me and after me are the very proof of. What is wrong with a little indulgence? In the name of God, didn't I sell enough of them?

Never forget that I was the Great Dictator not that old scoundrel de Valera.

Keep the book in print and to hell with the begrudgers who scream de mortuis nil nisi bonum, because believe me the dead are well capable of taking care of themselves!

Yours in Christ,

† John Charles

Howard Hughes, the world's most eccentric rich man, sends a postcard from Heaven to Ireland's least eccentric rich man, **Sir Anthony O'Reilly:**

Odd Balls Corner
Heaven

Tony boy,

The gurus have mournfully sung
Death takes the innocent young
The rolling in money
The screamingly funny
And those who are very well hung.

Yours,
Howard

Donogh O'Malley, former Education Minister and impossibly handsome playboy, writes to his nephew **Dessie O'Malley** with two things on his mind:

Dear Nephew,

Two things just for starters: One, it's never too late to go back to home base; and two, could you do something to salvage my romantic reputation? Would you not ask forgiveness and go back where you belong with the Party of Truth and Justice and abandon 'Trotters Harney' before it's too late. Forget standing down forever, for Jaysus sake man, and stand up. Get in there and spread some old-fashioned dissent among the Fianna Fáil backbenchers and you could be the leader in a month. Remember those great nights in Martin O'Donoghue's house? Remember you are the master at the heavy heave. Sure I'm not teaching my granny to suck eggs, am I? Limerick and the O'Malley clan abú!

On the other matter. Would you ever deny those feckin' rumours that I had bits on the side all over Dublin. You know I was the very model of the family man. Himself up here gets very upset when all those feckin' women start making claims that I fathered their feckin' bastards. For Jaysus sake boy, stand up for your auld Uncle Donogh.

As for the Arms Crisis nonsense, ignore it. Liam Ahern, who's sitting on the benches near me up here, was right: What we needed was guns. 'Bags of guns.'

Your loving uncle,

Donogh

Shergar, the world's most prime missing horseflesh, writes to one of Ireland's most distinguished and social jockeys, three-time Grand National winner, **Jason Titley**:

The Boneyard
Heaven

Jason me boyo,

What a great team we would have made, you and me. The crowds loved me and the crowds love you. Me auld bones have looked down from horse heaven and seen you struttin' your stuff over the years in those fashionable nightspots and all those prime fillies givin' you the eye. 'Tis mad jealous I do often be thinkin' how saddle sore you must be the mornin' after.

Fair play to you, boyo. I was sayin' to Arkle only the other night that Titley gives a new meaning to the phrase gettin' the leg over. By Jaysus, you wouldn't have to use the whip on that lot. Beecher's Brook is nothin' on it, boy. Says I to Arkle, if me bones are ever found I'll have my last restin' place called 'Mount Titley'.

Fair play to ya,
With respect and admiration,
SHERGAR

W. B. Yeats writes in verse – what else – to Ireland's most distinguished living poet, **John Montague**, on hearing that he has published a volume of autobiography:

Cast A Cold Eye Corner
Heaven

Come, receive our honoured guest:
Montague has done his best.
Let the Northern vessel by
Having poked us in the eye.

Fame, that with its strange excuse
Pardons Mahon and his Muse
And will pardon Heaney too
Fame is sure to pardon you.

Follow, poet, follow right
To the fag ends of the night,
With your booming Tyrone voice
Still persuade us to read Joyce;

With the farming of a verse
Make a rough field of the curse,
Sing of women who undress
In a rapture of distress.

Now that poetry's on the Dart
Give free expression to your art;
Instead of writing of your friends
Buy a drink and make amends.

101

Irish dramatist and wit **Oscar Wilde** writes to **David Norris**, gay activist, Joycean and Senator:

Pink Power Corner
Heaven

My dear Norris,

I write to you with the most grave intent. Let me be quite blunt. I have been quite irritated for some time by the misrepresentation in the Irish and international press that there was no homosexuality in Ireland until you came along with all that liberation business. (I simply cannot bring myself to use that appalling word 'gay'. In my day one was 'queer' or 'that way'. One was only 'gay' if one's horse won the Derby or one's team won at cricket.)

Be that as it may, I write on a wholly different mission. I want you to stand for the presidency of Ireland. I have had it in mind for some years now. It's about time there was a real Queen in the Vice Regal Lodge — I believe they call it the Áras these days. Good gracious, Norris, what does that terrible word mean?

The first thing I want you to do after your election – and believe me you will be elected, I have it on the highest authority – is change the name back to the Vice Regal Lodge. In fact that could be your main election plank.

I understand that the Phoenix Park is a haven for rough trade. I think that sort of thing should be encouraged. I mean to say, it provides excellent opportunities for politicians to meet their constituents. Well, Oscar is all for a bit of political 'wild life', but I think the trade should be warned not to get too close.

Now, be a good chap and heed old Auntie Oscar's advice. Post hoc, ergo propter hoc. In other words, 'take the ball on the hop and a hop to the Áras'. The idea of your elevation has much support up here amongst the gay republican brigade. I have bullied Casement and Pearse to write to you immediately.

I have the honour to remain,
Your adoring friend,

Oscar W.

Roger Casement, at the behest of Oscar Wilde, writes to support the election of Senator **David Norris** to the presidency of Ireland:

Disgruntled Heroes Corner
Heaven

Dear Norris,

I am not one to be bullied or harassed. Being ill-served by history is one thing but being bullied by buggers is quite something else. Who remembers 'lonely Banna strand' now except drunken faux republicans. I can tell you I had a bloody good time on that submarine journey.

Anyway I digress. Oscar Wilde has pursued me relentlessly to write you on the question of your assuming the role of head of state of our great republic. Personally, I don't give a tinker's curse who becomes head of state there or elsewhere but I want to get Wilde off my back and I'm terrified he will fulfil his threat of forging letters from me to you.

Oh my giddy aunt, I could not possibly suffer another forgery botheration. I can't suffer that

Wilde either. None of that limp-wrist poncing for me. T. E. Lawrence called me 'a broken archangel'. What do you make of that? I don't mind the 'archangel' bit, but I thought the 'broken' was a trifle rich. I can assure you I'm nothing of the sort.

By the way, I have no objection to being claimed by the 'gay' movement. I see they have my picture up in the gay bars in Dublin. Tell them I thoroughly approve. My only regret is I can't be there to do a bit of posing myself. I fancy I'd be quite a catch for the clones. I think I make a rather good role model for the young gay men of Ireland. It beats being a role model for scruffy, dandruff-laden, brown-envelope-taking politicians.

As for your presidential campaign you can say Casement is fully behind you, if you think that image won't frighten the punters or the horses.

Yours very truly,

Roger Casement

Patrick Pearse, poet, republican leader and aesthete, writes to **David Norris**:

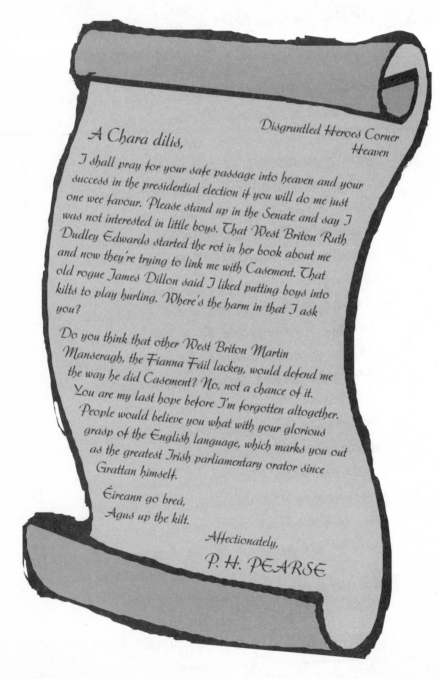

Disgruntled Heroes Corner
Heaven

A Chara dílis,

I shall pray for your safe passage into heaven and your success in the presidential election if you will do me just one wee favour. Please stand up in the Senate and say I was not interested in little boys. That West Briton Ruth Dudley Edwards started the rot in her book about me and now they're trying to link me with Casement. That old rogue James Dillon said I liked putting boys into kilts to play hurling. Where's the harm in that I ask you?

Do you think that other West Briton Martin Manseragh, the Fianna Fáil lackey, would defend me the way he did Casement? No, not a chance of it. You are my last hope before I'm forgotten altogether. People would believe you what with your glorious grasp of the English language, which marks you out as the greatest Irish parliamentary orator since Grattan himself.

Éireann go breá,
Agus up the kilt.

Affectionately,
P. H. PEARSE

Lord Lucan, the world's most famous missing Peer, writes to **Lord Henry Mountcharles**:

My dear Mountcharles,

Terrible luck, old boy. Now that old rotter Blair has abolished the hereditary peerage you're not going to get Daddy's seat. Frightfully tough on you, but then life was never easy for an old Harrovian living among the barbarians. I still have some ground rents there. The peasants are revolting but then they always were!

Clever of you to get all those rock folk up to Slane and bleed them dry. Wish I had thought of that one in the sixties. Old Jagger, old Bob Dylan, old Van the Man. Well, as somebody said, there is no stronger craving in the world than that of the rich for titles, except perhaps that of the titled for riches.

Oh, just in case there is any confusion, I'm quite dead, you know. Yes, and so is Elvis. Terrible business all that speculation about my being seen in South Africa, West Africa, West Cork. No quite dead, I fear. Well, that should give you something to talk about at Lillie's and those smart hangouts of yours. Yes, tell them that Lucky Lucan is just like the mother of Stephen Daedalus: dead, dead, dead.

Good luck old boy,
Yours ever,   Lucky

Brendan Behan writes from Heaven to his long forgotten biographer, Ulick O'Connor:

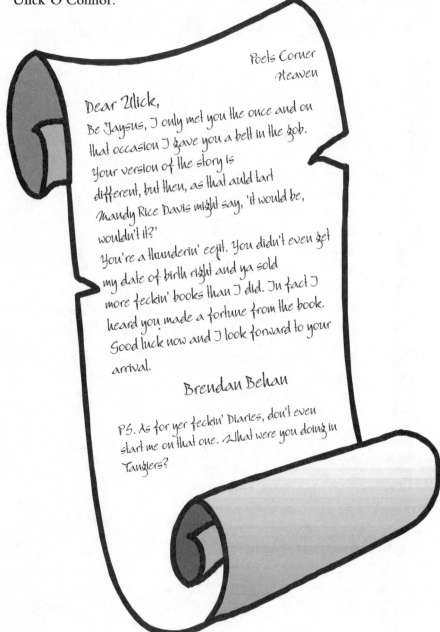

Poets Corner
Heaven

Dear Ulick,

Be Jaysus, I only met you the once and on that occasion I gave you a belt in the gob. Your version of the story is different, but then, as that auld tart Mandy Rice Davis might say, 'it would be, wouldn't it?'

You're a thunderin' eejit. You didn't even get my date of birth right and ya sold more feckin' books than I did. In fact I heard you made a fortune from the book. Good luck now and I look forward to your arrival.

Brendan Behan

PS. As for yer feckin' Diaries, don't even start me on that one. What were you doing in Tangiers?

The Rose of Mooncoin writes to the Rose of Tralee, Tamara Gervasoni:

The Kilkenny Shop
Heaven

Dear Tamara,

You looked great in the Dome at Tralee on stage with Marty Whelan in front of all those wild Kerrymen poured into tuxedos with their women out in their good frocks with their fake tans and fresh from the hairdressers.

Your orthodontist would be proud of you as your white teeth glinted at the cameras. Marty was lovely to you and flirted with you before you lifted your long green dress and danced a jig.

It's lovely that you want to travel the world and work with orphans. You will be a great ambassador for Ireland and will grace every reception you attend. The lads will flock to you like flies round a honeypot.

Isn't Marty gas all the same, although you would miss Gaybo. I'm only feckin' mad that the shower in Mooncoin didn't get their act together and then the RTÉ Outside Broadcast vans would be rolling into Kilkenny instead of parked permanently in the Kingdom.

With sashes and kisses and mind the cute hoors of Kerrymen.

Love
R. of M.

The authors of *The Annals of the Four Masters* write to the editors of
The Field Day Anthology, Volumes I–V:

Ladies and Gentlemen,

We have received here in Heaven five splendid and
beautifully bound volumes which contain the best of writing
by Irish men and women down the centuries. The first
three volumes came some years ago, ranging wide in time
and scope and purporting to record and present the best of
what Irish peoople throughout the ages thought and said
and wrote. Not much of a look in for Mná na hÉireann
in these finely bound volumes; presumably they were too
busy bearing and rearing children, running the house,
cooking meals, teaching the youth of Ireland, praying,
saving and listening and generally keeping the country
together while the menfolk blathered, boasted and
bellyached.

Now, just recently, to make tardy amends, former
President of Ireland and Best Bean an Éireann, has
launched volumes four and five of the completed Field
Day Anthology of Irish Literature. With great wit
and humour, compassion and magnanimity she spoke of the

treasure house these volumes contain in conveying the thoughts, perceptions, creations, songs, poems, stories and lore of the ignored and forgotten half of the Irish race.

'Better late than never,' muttered the male bastion of academia and The Irish Times. 'The mad women in the annex,' sniggered the drunks at the bar, 'next these feminists will be wanting the vote!'

Now we can all relax into our prejudices and presuppositions as the dust settles and we see Irish life and letters reflected as they really are at the beginning of the twenty-first century. It is like the Mass of olden days in Catholic Ireland – the men in their best suits on one side in three leather bound rows and the women kneeling, silent in their black lace mantillas.

So, Fir na hÉireann, let the womenfolk know what's what and who's who. Let them feel lucky they got in the door, even late in the day.

Nar leagadh Dia bhur laimh!
Beir bua ar an obair.

The Four Masters
(With not a mistress in sight!)

St Teresa of Ávila, saint of the Catholic Church, writes to **Donncha Ó Dulaing**, Corkman and RTÉ broadcaster:

Cloud Nine
Heaven

A Dhonncha, a chroí,

I want to thank you for all the RTÉ mileage you put up, following my cortège around the country last summer. You came up smelling of roses! You must have interviewed every bishop, priest, nun and auld wan in Ireland as my cortège and the casket moved through the country bringing the nation to its knees.

Thanks for the copy of the book, the CD, the holy water font, the beads, the joss sticks and the RTÉ Guide with me in the centrefold.

I'll put in a good word for you with Himself up here. Even though you have retired, there are no plans for you to reach the Pearly Gates yet. He tells a great Donncha joke: What's the difference between God and Donncha? (Give up?)

God is everywhere including Heaven. Donncha is everywhere except in RTÉ!

I'll be back for the return tour next year and I hope you'll join me for a cup of rosehip tea in the nuns' parlour, the Parlour of Dreams (yours).

Que Dieu et Son Mere Vouz Benir,

Teresa
of the Blooming
Roses

Jerimiah Newman, late bishop of Limerick, writes to the priests of Ireland:

Reverend Sirs,

The primary function of a priest is to keep his congregation awake. Or so says that frightful old atheist Peter Ustinov. I would say the primary function of a priest to keep his congregation in its place.

All very well for me, you may say; I was, after all, a true prince of the Church. I sent my silk underwear to Rome to be laundered, I collected vintage glassware, drank fine wines, rode to hounds, came from a good family, wrote my tracts on Georgian Ireland and my scholarly articles on the secular and the divine. A difficult act to follow for the average Joe Soap who drifted into the priesthood to escape the pigs in the parlour.

You all thought me arrogant and standoffish. How mistaken you were. Natural superiority will out no matter what. Have none of you read the history of the Church? Can't you follow the example of those who have preceded you? Of course not.

I mean to say that Casey man, the singing Bishop, fathering a brat by some American woman. Of course, The Late Late

Show (*LLS*) was the beginning and cause of his downfall. here he was sweating under the lights. (I heard the *LLS* also caused problems for Pee Flynn.)

I have no doubt that as you go about your daily task, you miss the true Churchmen like myself and John Charles McQuaid. 'Kiss my ring' should be the new philosophy of the Irish Church. Get the peasants down on their knees where they belong.

How happy you all were to mock me during my lifetime. Accusing me of being drunk when ringing up the RTÉ newsroom. Well, in the end you know, it wasn't the drink that killed me. It was the fact that I knew I would never be Pope. I admire the Pope, mainly because he tours without having an album or a CD.

There could of course be an Irish Pope one day (maybe only for one day) but that depends very much on whether you priests spend your time in the light with the five wise virgins or in the dark with the foolish ones.

I remain,

Yours in perfect humility,

†Jerimiah

Brendan Bracken, a former MP born in County Tipperary who was a pillar of the British establishment and was created First Lord of the Admiralty and Viscount Bracken of Christchurch by his old pal Winston, writes to **P. J. Mara**, Haughey and Bertie handler supreme:

Spin City
Heaven

Dear Mara,

I must say I admire your style. What a pity you didn't follow my example and head for the mainland as I did. You would certainly be Lord Mara of Cabra by now.

I was the greatest when it came to political handling. Have you ever seen the photograph of me giving out to de Gaulle? That is the sort of role a chap like you should have. You were not born to be in the background, hiding behind lesser men. You are not a handbag carrier, my dear Mara, you are a born leader. One leader, one voice. Let Mara lead on.

Now you see we have the spectacle of Manseragh sitting in the Senate. My family knew those Manseraghs. Half-mounted sirs we would have called them.

You, like me, are a man of the people. Take me as a humble example: I controlled the Financial Times, the Economist and the British government. There is no reason why you can't control the media and government of a nation of gombeens and half-wits. I issue the challenge. I lay down the gauntlet. Get a move on before it's too late. Don't you know moneyed half-wits and rock stars? Rob them blind. Don't hesitate. It's all for the good of the just cause of Mara. Mara's the man I say. Let Mara lead on. Put them out, to put Mara in.

Now is the time to recover from the years of humiliation and domination from that Mayo peasant Haughey. Charvet shirts, my ass. He wouldn't know style if it bit him. For God's sake, look at the mistress he took.

My dear Mara, by the time I next write to you, I expect you to have led the rebellion against Bertie of the Bowl and PD Mary, the farmer's daughter. Arrange for Seán Haughey to be the next FF leader and Taoiseach. You can then use the old posters — Let Haughey Lead On.

I shall pray for your success.
Your most devoted fan,

Brendan Bracken

P.S. We never recognised Tribunals. We always forgot to turn up; it's better to forget than to remember.

The **Lord God Almighty** writes to the man in charge in Ireland, Taoiseach **Bertie Ahern**:

Drumcondra Apartments
Heaven

Dear Taoiseach,

On Sunday evening 20 October Seán Lemass informed me that the Nice Referendum had been passed by a clear majority. I was so happy that your Government had ensured the majority that allows for the enlargement of Europe. At the moment you are Taoiseach of Ireland (TOI), but in time you will be Taoiseach of Europe (TOE).

Bertie, I want you to consider organising a referendum in your Ireland on my new policy proposal on Death. I am considering introducing a system whereby every person would receive one week's notice by post of their impending death. This new system would have many benefits, for example, it would give people:

1. *Time to get their 'affairs' in order.*
2. *Time to organise the 'going away' party.*
3. *Time to organise the funeral, which would take place at the end of the going away party, i.e. from the party to the graveyard at midnight and back to the party.*

As you would be organising the Referendum, it would show how powerful your contacts are in the next world while still TOI on Earth. Once the Referendum is passed, I can arrange with you that 'one week's notice of death' will become Fianna Fáil policy. I will also arrange that you can personally contact me by e-mail with a list of people (dissidents – you know what I mean) that you want called home to Heaven.

They will immediately get one week's notice, so make sure you always insist on two week's notice for parliamentary party meetings.

Of course, you will be rewarded for your role in ensuring that My policy is implemented through Fianna Fáil policy – how else could I achieve my aim, after all FF represents the heart and soul of Ireland. When your time comes to be called ashore I will give you five year's notice. I expect you to be TOE until the year 2060 when you will be 115 years of age. I will then call you home and have you immediately canonised as Saint Bertie of Drumcondra. What greater miracle can there be than for you to be Taoiseach for over 60 years. Of course, this is only possible when your opponents disappear from Earth with a week's notice.

I met old Ben Dunne at a garden party in Abbeyville Avenue Heaven yesterday. I told him of my plan, but he was concerned that people would mix up St Bertie with St Bernard. I told him to forget about those Better Value Stores in Ireland, or Thanks A Million Big Fella might be receiving rather than giving an envelope.

Once this new policy is in existence for 20 years I will then extend it to the UK (if it is still there). Tony Blair thinks he is God but, by the year 2022, you will be TOE and in a position to have him receive the appropriate letter.

Please consider the contents of this Very, Very Private, Confidential and Important Letter. Do not show it to anyone in the Department of Foreign Affairs, as it may be leaked to the media under the Freedom of Information Act. Contact me by e-mail at god@heavenanddrumcondradotdot.com.

Kindest regards Bertie,

Your Saviour